GOD
with Skin On

Finding God's Love in Human Relationships

ANNE ROBERTSON

www.godwithskinon.com

Morehouse Publishing
NEW YORK · HARRISBURG · DENVER

Morehouse Publishing, 4775 Linglestown Road, Harrisburg, PA 17112

Morehouse Publishing, 445 Fifth Avenue, New York, NY 10016

Morehouse Publishing is an imprint of Church Publishing Incorporated.

Cover design by Laurie Klein Westhafer

Library of Congress Cataloging-in-Publication Data

Robertson, Anne, 1959–
  God with skin on : finding God's love in human relationships / Anne Robertson.
      p. cm.
   Includes bibliographical references (p.   ).
   ISBN 978-0-8192-2311-1 (pbk.)
    1. Interpersonal relations—Religious aspects—Christianity. 2. Love—Religious aspects—Christianity. 3. God—Love. I. Title.
   BV4597.52.R63 2009
   241'.4—dc22
                                    2008052766

Printed in the United States of America

09 10 11 12 13 1410 9 8 7 6 5 4 3 2 1

To my genius brother, Rob,
who was the voice of God for my plays
and now is the song of God in my heart.
I love you.

Contents

Acknowledgments vii

Introduction ix

The Jesus in You 1

Section One: All In the Family 5

Are We There Yet?

    Relationships between parents and children 7

Mom Always Liked You Best!

    Relationships with our siblings 17

For Better or for Worse

    Relationships with our covenant partners 29

Over the River and Through the Woods

    Relationships with our extended families 39

Section Two: The Outsiders 47

I Get By with a Little Help

    Relationships with our friends 51

From Classroom to Cubicle

    Relationships with our peers 64

Yes, Sir!

    Relationships with authority figures 77

The Devil with Skin On

    Relationships with our enemies 90

Section Three: My Cat Found God on Facebook.... 103
God with Fur On
    Relationships with the animal kingdom 105
God on Facebook
    Virtual relationships 115
God without Skin On
    Relationships with the spiritual world 126

I Am the Way 137

Bibliography 142
Notes 145

Acknowledgments

I f any of you should ever again hear me utter the words, "I think I'll write a book about human relationships," please take me to a nice padded cell until the fit passes. Those of you who write know the terror of the blank page, but this book also gave me the terror of the printed page—the terror of having to face all of my own relationship demons and failures while trying to offer up something coherent for readers. There were some days when just writing the first page of a chapter brought up so much junk that I couldn't write for the rest of the day.

Since writing was much more difficult than I anticipated, I need to acknowledge the patience of my Morehouse editor, Nancy Fitzgerald, who was so gracious when I missed my first deadline. And then my second. I also need to thank my colleagues at the Massachusetts Bible Society who adjusted their work models so that I could work from home more frequently and have more energy to get the book finished.

I bear a debt of gratitude to those brave souls who first laid eyes on the manuscript to offer feedback and constructive criticism. They enabled me to make the book as good as it could be before sending it in. Annette Cerullo, Anita Conklin, Thom Gallen, Joan and Bill Humphrey, and Bill McWilliams all provided thoughtful responses that helped me make important changes and adjustments.

Lastly I want to thank all the people who have ever braved a relationship with me, both friend and foe. All of you have taught me something about life and love. Like Jacob after wrestling with the angel, I have come to this point with a limp but also with a blessing.

Introduction

A little boy reached that terrifying time of day when his mother would turn out the lights in his room and leave him for the night. Afraid of the dark and of being by himself he cried out for his mother to stay. Being a woman of faith, she reassured her son that God would be with him through the night. "But, Mama," he cried, "I need God with skin on!"

I don't know who first told that story, but it has endured because it speaks the truth. As human beings we exist in the world of human relationships and bodily experiences. Like the disciple we call "Doubting" Thomas, we need to touch God physically to believe God is actually present with us.

That is normal. It is so normal that God agreed to the unthinkable. God decided to put skin on and come to earth as a human baby, to grow into that skin as all people do, and even to allow his enemies to tear that skin apart with lash, thorn, and nail. Why? Because we as human beings have trouble with abstract concepts. Although we heard the teaching of Leviticus 19:18 to "love your neighbor as yourself," we argued about what that meant. We needed "God with skin on" to come and actually show us what it looked like in a real human life. Our salvation came to us in the flesh when we could not manage to bridge the gap ourselves.

There are many books written about that event, which Christians call the "Incarnation." Whether we use the language of the Gospel of John and call it "the Word made flesh" or the language of a little boy calling for "God with skin on," there is no shortage of material trying to sort through who Jesus was and what he accomplished in his life, death, and resurrection.

My focus here, however, is less on the actual life of Jesus and more on the basic truth that Jesus came to address—the truth articulated by a little boy facing the terrors of night: To really know God, we need to experience God with skin on. While the world may have needed the life and work of Jesus in a cosmic sense for one brief and shining moment in salvation history, I believe that we still need God in the flesh, day in and day out. God may have done a great and saving work back in the year 33 AD, but it wasn't enough to soothe the fears of a little boy in a dark room two thousand years later.

There is still a crying need for God to take on human flesh— every day in every place. That's where you come in. This is a book about you and the calling I believe we all have to embody God's love for others, especially those others with whom we are in relationship of one kind or another. This book is about Incarnation and the implications of being the Body of Christ. Here. Now. You. Me. All of us together. In relationship with God, self, and neighbor.

In these chapters we will look at the large variety of relationships we have, beginning with our families, moving out to our broader circle of non-family connections, and then, moving across the bridge of our relationship with animals and virtual relationships, we'll arrive at our ability to relate in the realm of the Spirit directly to God. We will then wrap it all up in a new interpretation of Jesus' famous claim to be "the way."

As we examine the relationships of our lives, we'll look at some psychological studies that reveal our human foibles as well as biblical texts and stories that may have either insights or warnings about how we relate to each other. Each chapter will then focus on what it might look like for us to be "God with skin on" in that relationship, ending with a set of questions either for personal reflection or group discussion.

I begin with the acknowledged bias that God is present in and through all human life and activity, whether that presence is acknowledged or not. The Bible begins with the assumption that God exists and seeks only to reveal God's nature and the means by which God works in human history. In the same way, I begin with the assumption that God is at work in human relationships and explore only how that might show itself and what we might learn about God and each other from it. If you believe in God, I hope to convince you that every relationship you have with friend or foe is connected to that divine relationship. If you don't believe in God, this probably won't change your mind—but I would like to offer one proposal for your consideration.

On a number of occasions I have run into people who have stopped believing in God because God did not show up and/or intervene in a tragic situation when needed. While the topic of why God allows horrible things to happen is beyond the scope of this book, I do hope that readers in such a place will consider that perhaps God did show up at those times. Was there a friend who stood by you? A doctor who made heroic efforts? A church member who brought a meal? A stranger who was able to provide a cup of cold water when your thirst was great? Were you telling your story to me, I would tell you that those people were God showing up. God in the flesh. God with skin on. And maybe that would make a difference.

The Jesus in You

You may be the only Jesus some people ever meet. That's the thesis of this book. God donned human skin in Jesus, which is a pretty wild thing to do if you already have all the perks of being God. But that radical act didn't end there with Jesus' death and resurrection. In fact, it was just beginning. The very last thing Jesus tells his disciples in the Gospel of Matthew is to go out and make disciples (Matt. 28:19) so that the work Jesus had been doing could continue. What work? The work of being "God with skin on" for others, the work of being the Body of Christ.

When Jesus was asked what the greatest commandment was (Matt. 22:36–40), he didn't pick one of Moses' top ten. He didn't even pick just one. He picked two: "Love the Lord your God with all your heart, and with all your soul, and with all your might" from Deuteronomy 6:5 and "Love your neighbor as yourself" from Leviticus 19:18. Out of the hundreds of laws he could have picked—laws about right behavior and idolatry and justice—Jesus picked the laws of relationship to be central.

In fact, Jesus went on to say, "On these two commandments hang all the law and the prophets" (v. 40). In other words, issues of relationship were, to Jesus, at the heart of every single bit of the Scriptures. Remember that Jesus taught in the Sermon on the Mount, "So when you are offering your gift at the altar, if you remember that your brother or sister has something against you, leave your gift there before the altar and go; first be reconciled to your brother or sister, and then come and offer your gift" (Matt. 5:23–24). Jesus is basically saying that there's no point in offering your gifts to God if the most important thing you have to give, namely your love, is being withheld from others. You think our church coffers are struggling now . . . imagine if we didn't take money from anybody who was in a conflict with someone else!

Paul echoes this notion that loving relationship is all that matters in his famous passage on love in 1 Corinthians 13. After saying in a number of ways that if we don't have love we're only so much noise, he ends with the incredible statement: "And now faith, hope, and love abide, these three; and the greatest of these is love." Sounds great at a wedding, but do you hear what he's saying? Love is greater than faith? Paul is very fond of faith as you can tell from his other writing, but he's very clear here that God's litmus test is not what we believe but whether we are capable of love.

We may sing in our churches "They will know we are Christians by our love," but in our practice we seem to want to identify ourselves as Christians by our political ideology, our church affiliation, our assent to creedal statements, or any of a host of other issues. But that's not what Jesus taught and that's not how Jesus lived. When God took on human skin to show us what God's Word looked like lived out perfectly in a human life, that life turned out to be focused on how to be in loving relationship, even with our enemies.

So for those who want to sign up for discipleship under this particular master, the first step is adopting the same priorities that

Jesus did: Love God with all you've got and love your neighbor just as much as you love yourself. When we are in loving relationship with God, neighbor, and self, the rest will take care of itself.

Notice that when Jesus gives a two-part answer to the question about the greatest commandment, he doesn't rank them. He doesn't say, "Well, first love God and then when you've got that down work on loving your neighbor." No, instead he tells us that the commandment to love our neighbors is "like unto" the commandment to love God. In other words, they are two ways of expressing essentially the same thing.

I think Jesus is saying that love of God is expressed through both the love of others and the love of ourselves. There's no point in falling into some ecstasy while singing "Oh, how I love Jesus" if we go home, kick the dog and scream at the kids. The first letter of John says that we're lying if we claim to love God but don't love a brother or sister (1 John 4:20). Jesus says in Matthew 25:31–46 that what we do to others we do to him. Love of God and love of neighbor are intimately linked.

If that is true, then issues in our own day-to-day relationships are not just a matter for the therapist's couch. They are part and parcel of our faith. When we fail to love, we have lost our witness to God's love in the world, making all our testimonies of faith sound like a noisy gong or clanging cymbal. When our relationships are damaged there is a danger that faith could be damaged, and if we harm another person, we have distorted the image of God for them in addition to whatever physical or emotional harm we may have done. Broken relationships are a matter for confession and repentance—not the kind of repentance that grovels in "I'm a worm" self-abuse, but the kind that gets up and does something about it.

The word "repentance" in the Bible means, very literally, to turn around and go the other way. The modern German word for repentance is *Umkehr*, which is also the word for a U-turn on the highway. When we realize a relationship has gone sour, repenting of that means doing something differently to work it out. Depending on the problem, "working it out" might mean ending the relationship entirely so that no more harm is done. It might mean working to be reconciled to the person, seeing a counselor to get your own head in order, or something in between. What it doesn't mean is wallowing in it and wringing your hands or ignoring it and pretending like everything is okay. When a relationship is on the rocks, faith is suffering—on both sides—and it's time to get to work to curb the damage.

That's what this book is about. These chapters are not meant to be a cure for your relationship woes. I'm not qualified to do that, and I doubt that a book can do such a thing. Believe me, I've read every relationship book out there and I still can't get it right. What I want to do is explore the ways that our various relationships might impact our own relationship to God and how our actions toward others can help or hinder their ability to find the God of Jesus Christ.

You may be the only Jesus some people ever meet. You are "God with skin on" in every relationship you have. That's a huge responsibility, but also an amazing gift with the power to help "Thy kingdom come, thy will be done on earth as it is in heaven." We may not get all the way there, but all of us can do a bit better tomorrow than we did today. When we do that, the God of grace will make up the difference.

Section

1

All in the Family

For good or for ill, we first learn what it means to be in a relationship from our families of origin. Most of us do our best, but most of us mess up on a more or less regular basis. Many of us did not have good role models growing up and we simply carry the only examples we know out into the complex world of interpersonal relationships. This is why therapy exists.

Our family bonds form some of our most basic attitudes, understandings, and beliefs. Before we can speak, we learn whether or not we can trust, and something of what love is. For those of us with siblings, it is there that we first encounter a peer relationship and decide whether competition or cooperation will be our way to success in the world. As we interact with parents we absorb lessons about authority and the use of power as they try to teach us the balance between responsibility and freedom. Our intimate partners teach us whether it is safe to be vulnerable to others and our extended family let us know whether there is a broader safety net if something close to home goes wrong.

Especially with family relationships, our language provides a bridge to Christian spiritual formation. Although the Bible uses *many images for God, the predominant one in our churches is that of a parent, usually a father. How often have you heard a fellow Christian referred to as "Brother John" or "Sister Renee"? I know if I had a dollar for every time I've heard reference to "our church family" I'd be living on my own island in the South Seas. I remember singing the old chorus, "I'm so glad I'm a part of the family of God." There's at least one hymnal called "The Family of God Hymnal."*

As a minister, I've had family roles imposed upon me. When I was young, the congregation saw me as a daughter and they tried to parent me. As I grew older, I became the congregation's spouse and then a mother to the congregation's children. One day, as I related my own inability to bear children, one adult church member said to me, "What do you mean? You have 550 of us!" (That's a bit much on laundry day!)

My point is that with family imagery so prominent in our churches, it shouldn't be surprising that we transfer experiences and expectations from our biological families to our church families and even beyond that to God. In some cases that might be a wonderful blessing that provides an incarnational way of understanding the love of God and our responsibility to others. In other cases, when our foundational family relationships have been significantly flawed, it might create major obstacles for knowing and receiving God's grace.

My experience in thirteen years of pastoral counseling has taught me that people are helped by becoming more aware of the ways in which family relationships can spill over into faith. We may still need years with a skilled counselor to help us with the residue of family issues, but maybe in recognizing the connection we can train up our faith to be part of the solution rather than part of the problem. So let's examine how that might work.

Are We There Yet?

Relationships between parents and children

During my first semester at seminary, my mother came for a visit. Just before she left to return home she asked me a rather odd question: "How are you set for your first church?" she asked. I had no idea what she meant. In the United Methodist system it would not be up to me to find a church; I would be appointed by the bishop. I was not going to be serving a church as a student and was several years away from the opportunity for either graduation or ordination, let alone walking into my first pulpit. What did she mean?

As it turns out, she meant finances. "Do you have a budget? Have you figured out what you will pay in taxes?"

"How am I supposed to do that?" I asked. "I have no clue where I will be sent, what my salary will be, or anything. It's three years away!" Then suddenly a light came on in my head. I saw not just my mother's question in the moment but the broader personality trait that it represented. A wry grin spread across my face and I said to her, "So, have you been this way all of my life? No wonder I have anxiety problems!" She laughed, the subject dropped, and I waited to figure out my taxes for my first church until I was actually appointed to my first church.

What I saw in that moment was the subconscious influence my mother's need to plan life years in advance had on me growing up. The answer was, yes, she had always been that way. As a result I absorbed her anxieties about the future. I wasn't joking. I did indeed have anxiety issues. Her neurotic planning gene was not the sole reason for that, but I would bet the farm that it played a role.

And then I thought about my mother's own mother, who ran off with another man when my mother was just a toddler. For a month no one knew where she was or what had happened. She just disappeared. Did my mother's anxiety stem back to the disruption of her own world at such a young age? Did she feel a need to plan out life so completely because her earliest memories held such panicked uncertainty about the center of her universe?

I was thirty-two years old at the time of my mother's tax question. It took that long for me to see my mother as a human being with her own set of fears and foibles from enough distance to consider how that may have impacted my childhood and who I became. Suddenly I was mourning the early loss of my father in a new way, realizing that I never had the chance to watch him with adult eyes and learn things about myself that vision might have brought. All I was sure of was that I had absorbed his warped sense of humor and was fearful enough of his censure when I kept him waiting that I have spent most of my adult life undoing my tendency to be neurotically early for events.

Don't get me wrong. I had a solid childhood. Both of my parents were kind, loving, well-educated people who gave my brother and me a home and an upbringing that many would envy. All I'm trying to do is to echo what psychologists have been saying since the science began: our parents have a humungous role in who we become.

Now theories differ about why that is. Some place more stress on biology and the genes passed along to us by our biological parents, regardless of whether or not they stick around to raise us. Others focus more on the "nurture" of the people, whoever they are, who have the greatest influence in the home. Freud is famous for focusing on the role of sexuality and attraction to mother or father, and Erik Erikson lays out a lifetime chart of psychosocial development and what traits are developed at each stage of human life. Everybody has his or her theories. But it would be tough to find a psychologist anywhere in time or space who didn't acknowledge that parents, both biological and otherwise, shape us both in ways we understand and in ways that we don't.

I'm not by any means the first to suggest that faith is also influenced in the cauldron of family life. In fact, these days all the theories of parental influence seem to be surfacing in regard to religion. Pretty early on, Erikson's developmental theory was applied to moral development by Lawrence Kohlberg and then specifically to faith development by James Fowler. Geneticists are now telling us that certain genes account for liberal or conservative leanings, and neurologists can describe religious faith in terms of activity in certain parts of the brain.

I look to what people in the churches I've served have told me. Women talk to me about abuse endured at the hands of their own fathers and how that has presented them with a gut-level revulsion when told that God is their "father." For some women the imprint of their early horrors is such that they simply cannot sit in a church that uses "father" language. For them it's not a matter of how Jesus referred to God or other biblical proofs. It's not about "*our Father*, which art in heaven," it's about *their fathers*, who many truly hope are burning in the fires of hell for what they have done.

But just shifting language to "mother" doesn't do it. That only sets off those who had abusive mothers. As one who believes that "God spoke and there was . . . ," I do believe that words matter. Word can become flesh and there is no such thing as "just words." However, the problem here does not have its root in language, and changing the language will not fix it. God as a parent—mother and father both—is an incredibly helpful metaphor. It only goes so far and it shouldn't be the only thing we use, but it can be a very helpful tool in understanding our relationship with God and God's concern for us. We don't need to find a better word. We need to become better parents.

THE BIBLICAL WITNESS

The Bible is full of parents and their children. There are the narrative stories we read about family life, especially the stories of the patriarchs in Genesis and the various battles over kingship and succession in the two Samuels, Kings, and Chronicles. There are laws about honoring parents and how to deal with disobedient children (it isn't pretty). The poetic books wax metaphorical about mothers, both human and animal, who protect their children and know them from before birth. Jesus makes distinctions between those whose "father" is God and those whose paternity stems from the devil. Paul gets very specific about the roles that family members should play in various circumstances.

Nevertheless, it is hard to figure out our contemporary parent/child issues from the stories of the Bible because the cultures represented there are so vastly different from our own. The story of Abraham's near sacrifice of his only son, Isaac, is so appalling to contemporary ears that more and more people simply cannot connect to the underlying truth it tries to teach us. Paul spoke to a world where women and children had no rights apart from their fathers or husbands. They were property, plain and simple. When we read of conquering nations making fathers watch the execution of their children, we see only the torment inflicted on a loving parent. The point in the culture, however, was to make a person aware that his or her legacy was being ended—that the only form of immortality they could envision, living on in their children, was being taken from them.

Even the stories of Jesus can give us pause as we sit two thousand years later in a culture so foreign to the biblical texts.

How could Mary and Joseph not notice that their twelve-year-old son was not with them as they traveled home? When Mary asks Jesus to help at a wedding that had run out of wine, his response to her seems disrespectful at best. When Jesus' mother and brothers show up to a gathering where he is speaking and want to talk with him, Jesus practically disowns them, saying, "'Who is my mother, and who are my brothers?' And pointing to his disciples, he said, 'Here are my mother and my brothers!'" (Matt. 12:48–49)

Of course this is the same guy who also said that his job was that described by the prophet Micah, "For I have come to set a man against his father, and a daughter against her mother, and a daughter-in-law against her mother-in-law; and one's foes will be members of one's own household" (Matt. 10:35–36). And then says in Luke 14:26, "Whoever comes to me and does not hate father and mother, wife and children, brothers and sisters, yes, and even life itself, cannot be my disciple." Nothing like a good dose of family values from the Savior! Jesus speaks in a different time, place, and culture.

The biblical parenting story that connects with us most is, ironically, the one that never happened. It is the story Jesus made up and told as a parable that we have come to call the Prodigal Son. Probably it was as difficult then as now to showcase a real family that could be an accurate reflection of God's amazing grace. The story is situated in Luke 15, which is sometimes called the "lost chapter" with its parables about the lost sheep, the lost coin, and ultimately the lost son—the Prodigal—in verses 11–32.

There are many facets to this parable, but here I want to focus on the father-son relationship. The basics of the story are these: Dad is wealthy and has two sons. At some point either at or nearing adulthood, the younger son demands that his father give him his share of the family inheritance early so he can go off on his own. This was a huge insult in its time, implying that the son considered his father as good as dead or wished him to be so. The father divides the property between his sons and within days the younger son takes off "to a distant country, and there he squandered his property in dissolute living." Who doesn't know that kid?

Well, pretty soon the lessons of economics he never learned hit home for the prodigal. Famine hits that distant country, his money is gone, and he finds himself tending pigs to earn a meager living. Knowing the culture here is helpful. Jesus is talking to Jews and presumably the family of the prodigal is Jewish, as Jesus says nothing to the contrary. If the prodigal is tending swine, he is obviously in a Gentile country and has made himself unclean both physically and spiritually.

What's worse, the pay he's getting for the pig-feeding job isn't enough. The prodigal is going hungry to the extent that he envies the slop he is feeding the pigs. Then it hits him. The servants back in his own house never wanted for anything. He knew that thumbing his nose at his father the way he did would make him persona non grata as a son, but maybe he could go back as a servant. He begins to practice his "I'm not worthy" speech to his father.

We'll get to that homecoming in a minute, but let's review what we've already seen of Dad's behavior. His youngest son delivers a grave insult by asking for his inheritance. Dad has lots of options at this point. He could lecture his son and refuse. He could give in with conditions and condemnation. He could boot his son out of the house penniless and give all the money to the eldest. He could give the money to the youngest and keep the eldest's share for the appropriate time. What did he actually do? "He divided his property between them." Nothing else is either said or implied. His heart must have been broken and perhaps he could see where his son's poor judgment would lead, but he let him make his own decisions and let him leave unfettered, treating both the "good" son and the "bad" son equally.

We don't have a picture of their family life before this point, other than knowing from the wealth that it was most likely a life of privilege. But the reflections of the prodigal in the pig sty on his life back at home show a household where servants were treated well, where they had "enough and to spare." Dad was generous, both with his sons and his employees.

There are many fathers whose sons would know better than to return after doing what the prodigal did, even as a servant. They would be toast if they dared to show their faces again and the sons know it. We can assume that this is not the first rash or hurtful thing that the prodigal has done in life, but his experience of his father thus far tells him that he would have a chance at being accepted back home into the servants' class, and that he would be treated well there.

Of course the prodigal was wrong. His father would not accept him into the servants' class. "But while he was still far off, his father saw him and was filled with compassion; he ran and put his arms around him and kissed him." The prodigal tries his "I'm not worthy to be your son" speech, but Dad will have none of it. He calls for the best robe and puts it on his son. He puts a ring on his finger and throws a huge and lavish party, "for this son of mine was dead and is alive again; he was lost and is found!"

This capstone to the series of "lost" parables in Luke 15 has a context. They are told in response to the Pharisees and scribes who are miffed at Jesus because "this fellow welcomes sinners and eats with them." Eating with someone in Middle Eastern culture, both then and now, is a sign of favor and acceptance. The importance of hospitality isn't nearly as pronounced in Western culture, but we do see some of the same issues in the political arena when people argue about whether or not we should sit down and talk with our enemies or whether a candidate should appear at certain schools, conferences, or interest groups.

The issue for the Pharisees at the beginning of the chapter is that sinners are bad and should be shunned. The point of Jesus in what follows is that sinners are lost and should be found.

While that distinction has profound implications for evangelism, the choice of a family story to illustrate Jesus' point highlights its importance for family relationships as well. What family does not have at least one prodigal somewhere? Maybe you have been that prodigal or maybe it was your son or daughter. Maybe you watched it play out with a niece or nephew, cousin or grandchild. Maybe there's an entire prodigal branch of the family.

In this parable, Jesus lifts up a father/son relationship to illustrate how God responds to us when we sin. We are allowed to make our choice, for good or for ill. We get what we ask for, even if it's not in our best interest. Then, when we are humbled by the realities of life and again seek our Father's face, he runs to greet us with a warm embrace before we can get a word in edgewise.

GOD WITH SKIN ON

The tragedy behind the Prodigal story is that there are too many real-life prodigals who have different experiences with their real-life parents. Some are wounded so badly early in life or sent away with such guilt that they never dare return to seek grace. Their experience has taught them that there will be none. Some return in hope and are turned away in shame.

From the father's side, some accept their prodigals home again and again, only to be insulted and robbed again and again. Some watch their children make choices from which there is no return, while others have the option to return but make a different decision. Real life is much more complex than the happily ever after of the parable.

So why tell it? I think because Christian faith is ultimately a hopeful faith. We recognize sin, but see in Jesus a way that sin can be overcome. Instead of shunning our sin, we are encouraged to find our righteousness from that sin's very depth. Like the bronze serpent that Moses put up in the wilderness, we are called to look the consequences of our sin square in the face in order to be healed. We hear the story of the Prodigal not as a fairy tale by which we escape reality but as a mirror by which we can adjust our lives.

How different parents and children look when viewing them through the glass of the Pharisees. We see the sin. We keep our distance. "They are bad. We will be tainted," says the Pharisee. Jesus whispers, "No. They are not bad. They are lost. I will find them."

That last part is crucial. It is God who will find them. We may or may not be involved in the search efforts. The bond between parents and children is, I believe, the strongest bond there is. That means it has the potential to inflict the most pain and do the most lasting damage. Parents who lose a child, of any age, never get over it. Many get through it, but they don't get over it. Likewise those who have been physically, sexually, or emotionally abused in the parent/child bond will always have those scars. With help and love they can heal over, but there will always be the scar.

There are times when the physical or emotional danger is simply too great for us to be the skin God inhabits to find a lost parent or child. I want to acknowledge that. God finds the lost sheep, sometimes through the mother, sometimes through the shepherd, who might be another family member but could also be a friend or a complete stranger.

But there are many other times when we are called to be God with skin on for our own parent or child. When you hold that new baby up to a mirror for the first time, see the father of the Prodigal standing behind you and adjust your image accordingly. Whether you are father or mother makes no difference, the gift of grace is not limited to one role or the other. Whether you want to be or not, you are God with skin on for that infant.

Dad, what your daughter comes to expect from you is what she will come to expect from God just as soon as she hears the words, "Our Father, which art in heaven." Mom, how you respond when your son gets drunk, crashes the car, and comes home with his head bowed low will not only determine whether he comes home again but also whether he will dare to face God when his sin has found him out.

And children, while your parents are figuring all that out, look past their image and see, as Harry Potter did in Dumbledore's magic mirror, the loving mother and father that God would be for you, whether you are the responsible elder child in the parable who did everything right or the prodigal who squandered it all. Both are treated equally. Both are welcomed at home. Both are loved. Even if your human parents have been more like the horrid Durselys, who made Harry Potter live in a closet under the stairs, look in the mirror and see your true father and mother. They are the shepherds who will find you when you are lost.

Being God with skin on requires both responsibility and grace. We won't always get it right, and getting it right won't mean that our children will never become prodigals. But for every time we do manage to be God with skin on for a child, there will be one more road home for her to travel when she grows up. And every time we look into God's mirror as a child we will see the one who has left everything to search for us.

DISCUSSION QUESTIONS

1. Who are your parents?
2. What personality traits do you share with those who raised you? Were they learned or did they just happen?
3. Did you learn about God in a direct way at home?
4. How is God like a father? How is God like a mother? Do you think of God differently if you use different words?
5. Have you been a biological parent or helped to raise a child? Has any part of the Prodigal story played out in your family?
6. Think of a time when you were God with skin on for a child, even if only in a small situation. Why did you do what you did? How could you do that more often or help others to do as you did?
7. Think of a time when you were a prodigal. Was anyone God with skin on for you? What happened? What was or was not God-like?
8. Have you ever had a hard time seeing past your own parents to the face of God?

Mom Always Liked You Best!

Relationships with our siblings

My brother, Rob, and I were out playing in the snow in our backyard. I suppose I was nine or ten years old, he two years my junior, and we were each engaged in our own pursuits with the once-fluffy white stuff that the warming sun and freezing nights had given a thick coating of ice.

I had my back to Rob, which is why I did not see him approaching with as big a sheet of ice as he could carry. I only noticed when he cracked the sheet over my back with all the strength he could muster. Perhaps I cried out a bit . . . I don't remember. But I didn't turn on him. I didn't run inside to tell our parents. I did dwell a bit on the fact that if he had hit my head and not my back, I probably would have been on my way to the hospital. But mostly I just continued to sit there, stunned, because although no violence had ever passed between us before, I knew why he did it.

In our very youngest years, all the pictures would attest to a very close relationship between Rob and me. I am hugging him as we sit side by side on a chair swing. We are chatting earnestly to each other on our respective toy phones. Perhaps that was a

myth created in pictures, but what I remember is that somewhere around school age, Rob became a problem for me. Which
meant I became a problem for him. Suddenly we were rivals.

It's not even clear to me what that rivalry was about, but suddenly everything the poor boy did was like fingernails on a black-
board to me. And so I whined and complained about his every
move. I teased and taunted and fooled him into thinking absurd
things in order to mock his ignorance. "Yes, Rob, snow falls up.
That's how you get white fluffy clouds." When in the fifth grade I
won the role of Lucy in *You're a Good Man, Charlie Brown*, I was
only playing myself. And so when his frustrations built to a point
that my mild-mannered brother (the brother who once went running in to Mommy crying that a wasp had stung him while also
sobbing, "He didn't mean to!") would bring an ice sheet down on
my back, I was able to have a moment of self-reflection.

No, his violence was not justified, but neither was my
taunting, although I don't remember moderating my behavior
because of that realization. But for some reason, once I went
off to college, the rivalry stopped just as mysteriously as it had
begun and Rob and I became friends. Over the years the relationship has grown so close that people have wondered if we
were twins. We now can communicate without speaking, have
frighteningly similar tastes, humor, and gut responses, and are
fiercely loyal to each other. I love him like no other, and this
book is dedicated to him.

Our story is lived out in millions of households with just
as many variations on the theme. Sadly, some rivalries intensify rather than fade and never come to resolution. Tragically, in
some cases when a sibling's frustration cup runneth over there is
a gun handy, the ice sheet finds a more vulnerable mark, or the
other sibling's taunting is much more violent or traumatizing.
Sometimes the rivalry emerges later in life, when siblings erase
the close bonds of a lifetime because of inheritance disputes.

Dr. Deborah Gold points out that because our siblings are
our first peer relationships, those relationships are where we

first learn about competition, cooperation, sharing, and getting along with others. That means that sibling rivalries don't generally remain only sibling rivalries. We are learning how to interact with others, and studies have shown those patterns can be transferred to other relationships—not just as children, but throughout life.[1]

If our sibling relationships can be displaced onto other relationships even a generation later, I would argue that they also can be displaced onto our faith-based relationships, both with God (who is so often portrayed as a parental figure) and with others in our religious community. As we discussed in the introduction to family relationships, the common "family of God" imagery in churches helps create a bridge over which both our positive and negative family experiences can travel.

Parents search far and near for help in dealing with their warring children, and there is certainly valuable guidance from psychologists out there. But what about the rivalry between "sister" Betty and "sister" Dinah, whose only relationship is in the church choir? Could it be that all the brother/sister church language has pushed old sibling rivalry buttons? How do we sort that out? I'm sure some of the sound psychological advice about siblings would transfer, but I think the Bible also has some wisdom to offer.

THE BIBLICAL WITNESS

Sibling rivalry in the Bible begins from the first minute there are siblings with the tragic story of the first brothers, Cain and Abel. In an apparent preference for meat over vegetables, God accepts Abel's sacrifice of sheep and rejects Cain's garden produce. Cain, the eldest, responds with the first human murder. As Abel's blood cries to God from the ground, Cain asks the immortal question, "Am I my brother's keeper?" Some might say that is the question that frames the entire Bible, and certainly the cultural prominence of the question helps ensure that human beings see each other as siblings, even outside of the bio-logical family.

Continuing in the Exodus narrative, we see power issues among siblings in Moses, Aaron, and Miriam. Throughout the stories of Israel's kingship there are stories of siblings vying for their father's throne, and in the New Testament Jesus has to step in as the sons of Zebedee argue about which of them is the greatest. Sibling rivalry is by no means a new thing.

Arguably the most famous siblings in the Bible, or at least the ones given the most ink, are the twin brothers, Jacob and Esau (Gen. 25–33). From the moment of birth, when Jacob is grab-bing at Esau's heel, and on into their adult lives, Jacob and Esau are fierce rivals. They are a therapist's nightmare, complete with parental favoritism—Dad loves Esau, Mom loves Jacob—and ever-escalating tricks and deceptions that finally bring Esau to his "ice-sheet moment" when he plots to kill Jacob. Mom finds out, alerts her favorite son, and arranges for him to skip town for a bit until it can all blow over.

But, just as modern psychologists might have predicted, Jacob's sibling relationship carries over into other places. As he goes to work for his uncle Laban, they too become embroiled in rivalry and competition, which extends to the two sisters that Jacob marries and goes on down to the handmaids of those sis-ters in a "who-can-have-the-most-babies" competition. Finally, in the same way that Jacob left Esau after the grand deception of stealing both the inheritance and the blessings of their father (who, remember, loved Esau best), Jacob pulls a similar stunt on his uncle Laban, taking Laban's flocks, herds, and daughters.

As Jacob takes his plunder and heads for home, the years of rivalry come to a head. The Jabbok River lies ahead. Just beyond that river is Esau with an army of four hundred men. Undoubtedly they would like a word with Jacob! While the ear-lier sibling rivalry was just between the two brothers, now these brothers have factions and supporters. The rivalry has grown and more blood is about to be spilled.

Of course Jacob is quick to develop a plan. Knowing that his flocks and herds, children, wives, and slaves are no match for four hundred men, he resorts to bribery. Jacob divides up his entourage into groups, sending each group out individually bearing gifts for Esau and his men. They are spaced so that just as soon as one group has finished presenting their gifts, the next group will be arriving. Maybe the first group will be treated harshly, but surely by the time they've been buttered up by group after gift-bearing group, all will be well for Jacob, who comes last with his wives and children. Or so he hopes.

Jacob also hedges his bets and prays. In Genesis 32:9–12 Jacob prays what might be seen as a "foxhole prayer." It is humble . . . "I am not worthy of the least of all the steadfast love and all the faithfulness that you have shown to your servant," but it is also made at the moment that he fears for his life. "Deliver me, please, from the hand of my brother, from the hand of Esau, for I am afraid of him; he may come and kill us all, the mothers with the children."

But whether the prayer is completely sincere or not, God steps in with one of the most interesting and mystifying stories in the whole Bible. God comes to Jacob as a wrestler. Jacob intended in his prayer that God change Esau's heart, and a part of me wonders what stories there were to tell on Esau's side that night. But God's direct answer to Jacob's prayer does not focus on changing Esau. God comes to change Jacob.

While the text is unclear about whether the actual wrestler is man, angel, or God, clearly the message at the conclusion is that the figure represents God in some way. The Bible tells us that Jacob and the angel wrestle all night there by the Jabbok River. There is mutual respect as they both do well, each besting the other in turn until a clever move by the angel puts Jacob's hip out of joint. The angel could have been declared the victor at that point, except that the angel then asks a favor of Jacob. "Let me go, for the day is breaking," says the angel. Jacob refuses unless the angel grants him a blessing. That, of course, is the way that

Jacob has always received his blessings—through manipulation of some kind.

All of which makes what follows quite strange. Instead of saying, "If you don't let me go I'll put more than your hip out of joint," the angel grants the blessing and says, "You shall no longer be called Jacob, but Israel, for you have striven with God and with humans, and have prevailed." This is completely odd. The angel clearly had the upper hand once Jacob's hip was dislocated, and yet he concedes the match, allowing Jacob to say that he beat God.

But the wonder doesn't stop there. The Jacob we have observed for the past eight chapters would have simply notched his belt and probably felt very clever. Not only could he steal his brother's blessing and inheritance and scam his uncle out of much of his wealth, he could also get God to concede a wrestling match. But that is not what we see. More than Jacob's hip is out of joint, it seems, and for the first time we see real humility in Jacob. Genesis 32:30 records, "So Jacob called the place Peniel, saying, 'For I have seen God face to face, and yet my life is preserved.'" *Peniel* in Hebrew means "the face of God." Jacob knows he didn't really win that match, and that God gave him something he didn't deserve. Jacob experienced grace.

While this wrestling match seems like merely a strange interlude to explain why Jewish law forbade Israel to eat the thigh muscle on the hip socket, I think it is much more. The wrestling match was God with skin on . . . God showing up as a rival and competitor to the one who had made rivalry an art form in order to show God's way in such circumstances.

And what is that way? Give it up. Let the other guy win, even if you're stronger and faster and clearly ahead. Seek to give a blessing rather than to receive one. When someone demands your cloak, offer your shirt also. The last shall be first. Die to live, lose to win. That is the way to peace. Always seeking to win has ultimately helped neither Jacob nor Esau. It has only escalated the rivalry to enmity and now possibly to war. There is another way shown by the wrestler-angel, a way that thousands of years later will be called the way of the cross.

Nothing could be more unexpected than the next part of the story. Jacob may have won his wrestling match, but his brother is still headed his way with four hundred men, and now Jacob's hip is out of joint. The bribes have gone out ahead and all that remains is the immediate family. Jacob and his wives went out bowing and groveling before Esau, expecting the worst. But, just as the angel did not take advantage of Jacob's weakness, Esau ignored all that groveling and "ran to meet him, and embraced him, and fell on his neck and kissed him, and they wept" (Gen. 33:4).

Now you can't tell me that such a response was Esau's intent from the beginning. You don't need four hundred men to hug your brother. But when Jacob bowed down and gave up the match to the brother he had bested in match after match, the rivalry melted away and Jacob was able to say in verse 10: "For truly to see your face is like seeing the face of God—since you have received me with such favor." The face of God. *Peniel* in Hebrew, which is what Jacob had just named the camp where he spent the night wrestling the angel and realizing, "I have seen God face to face and yet my life is preserved."

Jesus, of course, would have been steeped in this story growing up as he studied the Scriptures and learned of his heritage. I can't help but wonder if Jesus wasn't thinking of the amazing reconciliation of Jacob and Esau when he told the famous parable of the Prodigal Son (Luke 15:11–32). After all, the parable has an identical ending, as the father runs out to embrace the son who did so much wrong. Jesus implies that God is like the father. Jacob says that to see Esau's face is to see the face of God. They are both stories of God's radical grace.

GOD WITH SKIN ON

Of course the sad part is that although Jacob and Esau made up and came to realize the forgiving grace of God, their descendants did no such thing, and Israel and Edom (Esau's descendants) battled it out until there was no more Edom to battle. We do the same thing when we don't apply the lessons from Scripture to our own lives and relationships. Things that God worked out long ago are still things we battle—think of Japanese soldier Hiroo Onoda, who continued his WWII guerilla mission in the Philippines until 1974 because he didn't know the war was over.[2]

So how do we use Jacob and Esau to heal our rivalries? The turning point for the rivalry with Jacob and Esau is when Esau responds to his brother's surrender with grace rather than triumph and Jacob then makes the connection between that moment and his contest with the angel. Both Esau and the wrestler taught Jacob that there are other ways to use power. At long last it becomes about brotherhood rather than conquest.

Let's say you have two adult brothers who are not speaking to each other because one inherited dad's boat when the other brother knew dad meant him to have it instead. Until at least one of them comes to value having a brother over having a boat, the silence is likely to continue. That change of heart can come in many ways. It might come through spiritual development and learning to value people above things. It might come through a tragedy on one side or the other that helps put things in perspective. In cases like the early rivalry between me and my brother, it seems that what I needed was simply some maturity.

What is clear from the biblical story, however, is that although both sides may have been experiencing pain in the conflict, there were no assurances of how things were going to turn out. Jacob was completely vulnerable and knew his brother might whip out a sword and cut him down. But Jacob did not approach Esau as a warrior coming to battle. He approached as a servant. It is the attitude that King David reflected in Psalm 51:4 when he wrote, "You are justified in your sentence and blameless when you pass judgment." It is the attitude of repentance.

But it is not Jacob who represents the face of God in this story. Repentance is frequently if not always a necessary component in healing such rivalries, and if we know deep down that we are at fault, we should run, not walk, to admit our guilt. Scripture calls for this more times than I can count. But if we want to go a step further and be the Body of Christ—to be God with skin on for others—we have a different, and harder, task.

It is very hard to admit that we have not acted according to our better angels, whether our misdeeds have been great or small. But it is harder still to give up our right to pass judgment on someone who has wronged us. Yet that is the example of grace. Grace, by definition, is not something we deserve. It is the experience of receiving treatment that is better than we deserve. If I'm stopped for speeding, receiving a ticket is justice. Receiving a warning is grace.

Grace is what is embodied in both Esau and the father of the Prodigal as they rush to welcome with a kiss the ones that should, at the very least, pay substantial fines. Both Jesus and the man who fathers the nation of Israel declare that this radical grace is what the kingdom of God is like—that what some would say is a clear violation of justice is, in fact, the face of God. And that is where we come full circle back to our family relationships, and where the extension of family language beyond our biology can heal as well as hurt.

If the studies are correct, we are more than likely to bring our conflicted sibling relationships out into the world with us. It's a fair bet that sister Betty and sister Dinah from our earlier example, who compete bitterly for choir solos and who get offended if the pastor seems to prefer the baked beans of one over the other at church suppers, had similar rivalries with siblings growing up. But it is also possible that if sister Betty was willing to sit out the next solo audition and could swallow hard and suggest to the choir director that sister Dinah's voice was just right for that piece, that cries of "Peniel" might just break out in that choir. And maybe if sister Dinah received such grace after wrestling with angel Betty, she might carry some of that wisdom back to her biological sister and become the face of God herself, God with skin on for another.

Of course there are countless variations on the theme. In cases like Dinah and Betty, there is often enough immaturity and blame to go around. There are times when all of us need to just grow up, take our egos off their pedestal, and let someone else shine for a change. But sometimes, when there has been real hurt and abuse in a relationship, the waters of reconciliation are more treacherous.

Notice that with Jacob and Esau, it was the victorious rival who took the humble position. If Jacob tried to blame Esau for the conflict and played the "Woe is me, you have all these men and I'm just a weak sibling trying to make it home with my family and flocks, look how mean you are. That's why Dad gave me the blessing" card, that would have been just further abuse. While Jacob is outmatched in this moment by his brother's army, he has still taken more from Esau than can be regained even if Esau cuts Jacob down on the spot. Jacob is in a bad place at the moment, but he comes to that moment as the rivalry winner.

The reason that this meeting is a model of God's grace is because it was the victor who humbled himself before the one who had been wronged, announcing a willingness to take a lesser station—to be a servant of the one he had previously mastered. It is an acknowledgment that righteousness trumps might and craftiness every time.

By connecting this story with the face of God, the Bible bears witness that this is how reconciliation with God happens. We may have gotten away with all kinds of things. God did not stop us, and maybe some have mocked God as being weak for not putting a stop to our inappropriate behavior. But on the day we realize our error, we need not fear God's response. When we return with humility, God runs to meet us.

This also gives us a road map for reconciliation with others, whether we are the one who has behaved badly or the one who has been wronged. If we are at fault, we should fess up. Even if the blame can be shared, we should admit our part. And if we are to be God with skin on for others, when someone comes to us with that sort of humility, we should offer grace.

I want to be very careful here. Notice that Jacob does not come back saying, "I'm so sorry—I didn't mean it. I'll never do it again, now let's go back to the way it was and pretend nothing ever happened." This can be just another way that an abusive person weasels his or her way back into a relationship to do more harm later. Jacob is truly willing to come back in a servant's role and understands that Esau would be completely justified in refusing the overture. There is no "blaming the victim," but even after the warm embrace from Esau, the brothers do not return home arm in arm.

Reconciliation doesn't always mean the restoration of the way things used to be. That may or may not happen according to the circumstances. Reconciliation means that old wounds are no longer inspiration for new harm, and that two people who were at war have found peace. Lessons are learned and the parameters of a new relationship are forged from that experience. We may or may not have further contact with those people. The lessons from the experience might have included the need to protect ourselves from those who harm despite their best intentions. Or we might have learned that the brother we shunned as a human abnormality in our youth is our new best friend. What we accomplished in the reconciliation is simply the peace to make a clear and loving decision about what the relationship will look like moving forward—a peace that truly does pass all understanding.

DISCUSSION QUESTIONS

1. Did you have siblings growing up? Were there tensions? Were they resolved?
2. Do you think that talking about other Christians as our brothers and sisters brings in a family dynamic? Does that help or hurt?
3. Have you known siblings who have kept their rivalry into adulthood? What was it about?
4. Have you known siblings who worked out a rivalry and are now close? How did that happen?
5. What does it mean for a parent to treat children equally? How have you seen that succeed or fail?
6. What do you think the relationship of Jacob and Esau was like once they got home?
7. Have you ever seen one sibling be "God with skin on" for a brother or sister? What made it God-like?

For Better or for Worse

Relationships with our covenant partners

At every wedding I conduct, I explain to those assembled that we have such ceremonies in a church because a couple's love and commitment to each other are a witness to God's love and commitment to us. Every couple will have human challenges, to be sure. But how they handle those human challenges is a statement about who God is and how God behaves. Think of that the next time the trash doesn't go out on time.

I am also fond of quoting one of my favorite Broadway show lines. From *Les Misérables*, which I think is the best sermon ever put on a stage, we hear the words, "To love another person is to see the face of God." In one sense, that's what it means to be God with skin on in every type of relationship—to learn to see God's face in the other and to be as much of a mirror of God's face in our own lives as is possible for us to be. But I think that concept is supremely lived out between those who have entered into a partnership that is marked by a covenant before God.

Marriage is a complicated business in today's American culture. Of course the same-sex marriage question has been front and center, but it's not the only issue out there. There are those who want to commit themselves before God but for various reasons don't want to make that commitment a legal matter. There are those who have a legal piece of paper saying they have married, but who feel more of a commitment to the piece of paper than to their spouse. One man I knew had neither seen nor spoken to his wife in over five years. They lived in different states, but he didn't want to get a divorce because he didn't think God would approve.

Of course some people never make that kind of commitment in the first place. Since I am online more frequently than not, I've come to be familiar with much of the language associated with online chat. But when I ran across someone talking about their "fwb," I was mystified. As it turns out, "fwb" means "friend with benefits," which translates further into a friend with whom you have a sexual relationship but no commitment.

There are also those who remain "single" in terms of a romantic relationship but pledge themselves to other kinds of commitments. It's not an accident that those in religious orders take vows before God and wear a wedding band to show their marriage to Christ. There are the vows of ordination, oaths of office or profession, and sacrificial commitments to other causes that we signify in various ways.

For those reasons and more, I didn't want to rely on the word "marriage" to describe the relationships in this chapter. I don't want the main point to be lost in the various controversies. But I do think it's important that we talk of intimate relationships in terms of some sort of covenant—a promise with fairly universal standards that we make before others and solemnize in various ways—so I settled on "covenant partners."

To begin with, I want to consider why a covenant of any type is important. Promises can be tough to keep and cause a lot of grief when they fail. Why not just do what the "fwb" folks do and not worry about it? After two unsuccessful marriages of my own, it is quite tempting just to scrap the whole idea. Honestly. I thought about it a lot. I thought and I prayed and I read every blessed relationship book on the rack. It was, however, the Bible that taught me the most.

What I finally saw there was this: It's about faithfulness. By learning to be faithful to each other, we learn to be faithful to God. We are encouraged to seal our desires in a covenant partnership in order to proclaim to the world the nature of God's faithfulness to us. In doing so, we also develop our own capacity to be faithful, which will help ensure our faithfulness to God. I'll spell that out more later in the chapter, but first I want to turn back to the Bible to explain how I got there.

THE BIBLICAL WITNESS

As I mourned the loss of my first marriage and watched my husband marry another woman, I tried again and again to find solace in the Bible. Then, one night, my reading brought me to Isaiah 54. Since one of the tears in our marital fabric had been my inability to bear children, verse 1 immediately caught my eye: "Sing, O barren one who did not bear; burst into song and shout, you who have not been in labor! For the children of the desolate woman will be more than the children of her that is married, says the Lord." I was hooked.

The words of comfort go down to verses 5–6 where they intensify with "For your Maker is your husband, the Lord of hosts is his name; the Holy One of Israel is your Redeemer, the God of the whole earth he is called. For the Lord has called you like a wife forsaken and grieved in spirit, like the wife of a man's youth when she is cast off, says your God." I cried with gratitude and relief—great hulking sobs that went on through much of the night.

When I could get enough distance to analyze that experience, I realized that the image of God as a spouse is a primary one in the Bible. In the New Testament we read that the Bride of Christ comes down out of the heavens as the new Jerusalem (Rev. 21:2, 9) and Paul states directly that his dictates about husbands and wives are really referring to the relationship between Christ and the church (Eph. 5:32). But we get a much more specific picture of the connection between our human partners and our divine partner in the Old Testament where, in addition to countless other references, two entire books are dedicated to the theme: the Song of Solomon and Hosea.

The Song of Solomon is eight chapters of lovely, poetic, soft porn. That is to say, it is unabashedly sexual—every last chapter of it. It celebrates the nuptials of King Solomon and an unnamed woman. (Solomon had some three hundred wives, so that doesn't exactly narrow the field.) Whoever she is, she is madly in love with Solomon, who returns the favor as they chase each other around Jerusalem on their wedding day. The traditional interpretation justifies its inclusion in Scripture by saying that it is really about the relationship between God and God's people, although the book itself makes no such claim.

Even more telling is the book of Hosea. Consider God's opening command to the prophet in Hosea 1:2, "When the Lord first spoke through Hosea, the Lord said to Hosea, 'Go, take for yourself a wife of whoredom and have children of whoredom, for the land commits great whoredom by forsaking the Lord.'" So Hosea does exactly that. Again in 3:1 we read, "The Lord said to me again, 'Go, love a woman who has a lover and is an adulteress, just as the Lord loves the people of Israel, though they turn to other gods and love raisin cakes.'" I'm not quite sure what raisin cakes have to do with it—I'm guessing they were a common offering to the other gods of the time—but you get the drift. The whole organizing metaphor for the book of Hosea is to compare the wayward people of Israel to a wayward and unfaithful spouse. Adultery and idolatry are linked.

But it isn't just the prostitution of faith that gets attention. Faithfulness to God is also linked to faithfulness to a spouse. As God talks of Israel's return to faithfulness, the metaphor is still at work. In Hosea 2:16–20, "On that day, says the Lord, you will call me, 'My husband,' and no longer will you call me, 'My

Baal.' For I will remove the names of the Baals from her mouth,
and they shall be mentioned by name no more. I will make for
you a covenant on that day with the wild animals, the birds of
the air, and the creeping things of the ground; and I will abolish
the bow, the sword, and war from the land; and I will make you
lie down in safety. And I will take you for my wife forever; I will
take you for my wife in righteousness and in justice, in steadfast
love, and in mercy. I will take you for my wife in faithfulness;
and you shall know the Lord."

One of the most hopeful parts of the metaphor as it is used
in Hosea is that, when it comes time to talk of Israel's return to
faithfulness, Hosea accomplishes that with the faithless woman
first chosen. Hosea is not told to go out and find a virgin whose
heart is true or a widow who was faithful to her husband in
order to portray faithfulness. The one who has been unfaithful
is forgiven and is brought back into covenant relationship.

Throughout both the Old and New Testaments, God makes
promises—both to individuals and to peoples. That's a key part
of our understanding about the nature of God. This is a God
who both makes and keeps promises, which is why Paul spends
so much of the book of Romans trying to show that God's promise to Israel has not been abandoned just because God made new
promises to the Gentiles. The "new" covenant is *in addition to*,
not a *replacement for*, the "old." To me that means that our own
lives should bear witness to the faithfulness of God's promises
by being faithful to the covenants we make with each other.

If you line up the Ten Commandments on two tablets of five
commandments each, at least with the Jewish and Protestant
numbering system, the adultery commandment and the idolatry commandment are in the same position on their respective
tablets. I think that is a subtle reminder of how one of our most
important human relationships connects to our relationship with
God. In learning to be faithful to a human partner, we are model-
ing faithfulness to God and developing a virtue that will hold our
allegiance to our divine partner, even during the tough times.

As we deal with the betrayals of intimate covenant in our own lives, we should not lose sight of that. While God does not approve of our infidelities by any means, God keeps up God's end of the covenant to stick with us as the Anglican Book of Common Prayer has asked couples for centuries to vow to stick with each other, "for better for worse, for richer for poorer, in sickness and in health." We may bear a stigma with our human spouse or with other people, but we are always welcomed back into the arms of God.

GOD WITH SKIN ON

A married man in a congregation I served once asked me if it was possible to be in love with two women at the same time. My answer was, "Of course. But the covenant you made to your wife was not about whom you would feel warmly about in the future. It was about being faithful to her alone."

Love does play a role in the life of a healthy couple. But when love leads to our decision to seal that love in a covenant, we have moved to a new level. When we decide to make a promise before God that our loving actions, both sexual and non, will be directed toward one particular person, we are making a statement about more than the degree of our love. The biblical metaphors make clear that we are making a statement about the nature of God.

When we abandon that promise of faithfulness, we are claiming that God is not faithful, which harms both our witness and potentially the faith of our partner. When we fail in faithfulness, we have failed to be God with skin on. Not only does that cause the enormous feelings of betrayal and anguish in the injured party, it does damage to that person's ability to trust the promises of God.

I've told the story elsewhere of Carol, a divorced woman in her forties who came to me for pastoral counseling. She had been taking a class I was teaching and was struggling with a question asking her to name a time when she felt loved by God. Despite being a faithful church member for many years, she could not name a single time, which troubled her deeply.

The breakthrough in our time together came when she realized that in the wake of her divorce she had walled out not just the love of other men, but all love, to avoid experiencing that hurt again. After a few minutes of sobbing, a smile crossed her face and she went bouncing out of my office. She came in thinking God didn't love her. She went out realizing that her experience of divorce had led her to unwittingly keep God out. With that wall down, God's love shone brightly.

It was that experience and others like it that formed the seeds of this book. God's promise to Carol never wavered, but she doubted it because the one who was God with skin on for her gave a different witness. That was not conscious on either his part or hers. Her husband never said anything even remotely like "I don't love you and God doesn't either," although unfortunately there are cruel people out there who actually do say such things. But in her case, the connection between Carol's divorce from her husband and her divorce from God was all under the radar. Seeing the connection did not remove her distrust of men; she will have to work through those issues in other ways. But bringing that unconscious shift to light did allow her again to have the strength of God's love in working them through.

Those are the realities of human nature and emotion that underlie the strength of Jesus' admonitions against divorce. This covenant-making God designed human beings in such a way that our truest nature will proclaim God's nature. Not only do the heavens declare the glory of God, as Psalm 19 tells us, but human behavior, when guided by the will of God, is a witness to God's nature, bringing all of Creation together to proclaim God's love and faithfulness.

The highest expression of this is in our covenant partnerships, where we are completely vulnerable to each other in the perfect trust that our partner will bear with our fears and our failings with steadfast love. That is the relationship that God wants to have with us, even more than parent to child. Whole books of the Bible illustrate that.

While I didn't have that much of an understanding at the time, when I decided to end my second marriage (ending the first was not my choice) I was keenly aware of the ways that my decision could impact those in the congregation I was serving—especially the youth. I had many sleepless nights worried that as a pastor I would seem to be making a statement that marriage could be taken lightly and easily discarded. As a result, I stayed several months beyond the point where both my counselor and his told me I was in physical danger. It wasn't until I saw that I was becoming unable to fulfill my calling to preach the Gospel that I decided to leave.

I don't believe that my final decision to end the marriage was God's will for the union at the beginning. I do believe that, when it became obvious that our marriage could not be a witness to God's love and faithfulness, it was right to declare it to be a false witness and end it—both for my sake and for his. Continuing in a relationship that is designed to help us learn how to be both vulnerable and faithful to God when what we experience is counter to both of those things is destructive. It does psychological harm, it does spiritual harm, and it does harm to our witness in the world.

Brain trauma from a fall ended his life in 2007. At the funeral, while I felt the heartache of his family whom I love, I also found a sense of peace in learning that in the last years of his life he was able to be reconciled with both his family and his church, covenants that called to him from well before the time he made a covenant with me. Would either of us have found such peace if we had stayed together? It's hard to know, since I chose another path. But I do believe that he found the road of faithfulness in returning to church and family and I found it in being faithful to my calling. God worked it out, despite our various failings. Which brings up another issue.

As I mentioned earlier, one of the other reasons I wanted to talk about "covenant partnerships" rather than "marriage" in this chapter is because some of us, for innumerable reasons, never marry. Others choose to remain single after a breakup. While I think God designed marriage as a primary way for us to learn how to be faithful, it is not the only way. For those of us who, either by choice or by circumstance, have no "significant other," there is still the need to learn the virtue of faithfulness and to witness to the faithfulness of God.

As I mentioned above, my covenant partnership in marriage could not do that for me. But my covenant with my calling to preach the Gospel could. When I was fourteen years old God said, "Preach my love for the rest of your life." It was faithfulness to that calling that pulled me finally to seminary when my first husband left me, and I solemnized the covenant at my ordination. It was faithfulness to that calling that enabled me to end my second marriage. It was faithfulness to that calling that enabled me to bear up when people told me I was evil for daring to step into a pulpit as a woman or threatened bodily harm when I opened the door of a church to a black member. It was faithfulness to that calling that led me to move from parish ministry and preaching in one church to a position where I can preach in many.

That is just one kind of covenant partnership besides marriage. There are other forms of service and ministry in the world. There is the covenant we make through our baptism to become a living witness to God's love. There are vows made to country when entering military or public service. Other professions require oaths to administer justice or to seek healing and not harm. Personally, I think it's time to demand an oath from those entering the world of finance.

While everyone has such a calling regardless of the human relationships they have or do not have, for those of us who are single, I think the burden is greater to figure out what our primary commitment is and to solemnize our covenant with it.

We serve a covenant-making and covenant-keeping God. We serve a God who promises to love us for better or for worse, and has borne that out through some pretty bad "worsts." When we make human covenants, we are becoming God with skin on in that covenant relationship. While our human failings are bound to show, Jesus makes it plain that our humanity is not supposed to be an excuse for not trying. We can do better. With God's help we can keep more covenants than we break, and with God's help we can transform even the broken ones into a prism to show the facets of grace.

DISCUSSION QUESTIONS

1. What do you think is the difference between a relationship and a covenant relationship?
2. Have you ever felt betrayed by someone who broke a promise to you?
3. Have you ever felt it was necessary to break a promise to someone else? Why?
4. Right now, what covenants do you have? What are the challenges you face in being faithful to them? What makes it easier or more difficult?
5. Have broken promises ever affected the way you felt about your faith or your church?
6. How should a couple decide whether or not to solemnize their relationship with a covenant?
7. How could your faith community be more supportive of covenant relationships? In what ways are they already successful? What needs work?

Over the River and Through the Woods

Relationships with our extended families

Immediate families are confusing enough. When you start extending outward to grandparents, aunts, uncles, nieces, nephews, and cousins, most people have enough entertainment for a circus. Throw in the in-laws and a reality show can be yours for the taking. Sometimes that show is a crime show. Sometimes it's a dark tragedy full of secrets. Often it's just a cacophony of characters strange enough to populate a Star Trek episode.

My own extended family is relatively small, and yet still there are the stories. My grandparents (as well as my great-grandparents) liked marriage so much that they did it fairly frequently, with my maternal grandmother taking serial monogamy to new heights. As a result, I remember responding to my kindergarten teacher's question about how many grandparents I had with a number that was much too large. It turns out that my maternal grandmother wasn't actually so big on the monogamy part, and I remember the day in high school when a stranger called my mother and claimed to be her sister. Sure enough. Seems my grandmother neglected to pass along that little bit of information.

There were the Thanksgiving dinners that seemed to be a constant battle over social issues, the tragedy of my closest cousin's sudden death, the uncle in Vietnam, making the family rounds at Christmas, my paternal grandmother who babysat for Rob and me, always falling asleep in a child's rocker in front of the TV. Great Uncle Charlie only had four fingers on one hand. He would pretend to lose the missing finger in my brother's ear. You have your own stories that rush to mind in a din of memory.

Growing up, the closest emotional connection I had with an extended family member was also the closest tie that my father had. Aunt Anne. She was my great-aunt, and I was her namesake. If there was something not to love about Aunt Anne, we never knew it. She lived in another state, but we visited at least twice a year, called her every week, and sent many, many letters. It has only been in recent years as I have gone through my father's old letters that I have seen how much Aunt Anne served as a confidante for my father when he was a young man.

When he argued with his parents about his life choices, he turned to Aunt Anne for solace and understanding. And she gave it, both to him and to his parents. As the fog of Alzheimer's began to invade in her later years and she asked the same questions repeatedly on our weekly family phone calls, she finally said, "Isn't it wonderful? I always get new news and you never have to think of anything different to say!"

In many ways, Aunt Anne was the glue that held our family together, and many families have such a person in their extended network. Sometimes that person becomes an actual part of the nuclear family as grandparents end up raising their grandchildren or cousins move in and become siblings, which is not unlike what we see in the Bible.

THE BIBLICAL WITNESS

While there are plenty of troubled extended family relationships in Scripture, there is one that stands out as a shining example of how God can use extended families: the story of Ruth and Naomi. Their story, as told in the book of Ruth, begins in complete tragedy. Famine drives Naomi, her husband, Elimelech, and their two sons from their native Bethlehem to the country of Moab.

While in that foreign land, Elimelech dies. The sons marry Moabite women, Ruth and Orpah, but the two sons also die within the decade. As a widow who has also lost her two sons, Naomi is not just in deep grief, she is destitute. Women in that culture had no means of support without a husband or sons. So she decides to return to her native land, where the famine has eased. Ruth and Orpah start to go with her, but Naomi encourages them to stay in their native Moab where they are more likely to find husbands among their kin.

Orpah returns home, but Ruth will hear none of it. Her devotion to her mother-in-law runs so deep that her words are often used at weddings: "Do not press me to leave you or to turn back from following you! Where you go, I will go; where you lodge, I will lodge; your people shall be my people, and your God my God. Where you die, I will die—there will I be buried" (Ruth 1:16–17a).

Ruth is true to her word. She follows Naomi back to Bethlehem, and although the Moabites were not generally welcomed in Israel, Ruth becomes something of a local legend because of her devotion to Naomi. Naomi proceeds to act as a surrogate mother for Ruth and works to find her a husband among Naomi's own kin. The story of that effort and the resulting marriage to Boaz is the stuff of the rest of the book.

This story of faithful devotion earns its place in Scripture because of the progeny of Ruth and Boaz. They have a son named Obed, who is counted as a child of Naomi and for whom Naomi serves as a nurse. Obed becomes the father of Jesse, whose youngest son, David, becomes King of Israel and the ancestor of Jesus. Mothers are not usually mentioned in biblical pedigrees, but Ruth is mentioned in Matthew's genealogy of Jesus (Matt. 1:5).

GOD WITH SKIN ON

I probably don't need to tell you that while Ruth's words are often spoken at weddings, I have yet to do a wedding where they were spoken by the bride to her mother-in-law. Seldom is that relationship so close. But the book of Ruth reminds us that our extended family—the in-laws and the outlaws as it were—are part of God's plan for us. As with our nuclear family, sometimes they help, sometimes they hurt, or sometimes they just provide comic relief. But the potential is there for them to be God with skin on for us, as Ruth and Naomi were for each other in their time of need.

Whether we properly view God as an extended family member can be debated, but I think there are times when that image applies. In the negative sense, sometimes God serves as the crazy uncle for us. God is acknowledged as part of the family but is someone we keep at arm's length because we're not quite sure we want others to know about it. Sometimes being religious is treated as the family's dirty little secret, or at least something that is not shared in polite company.

Other times we don't view God so much as a crazy uncle than as a distant cousin. Unless God actually shows up and knocks on the door, we kind of forget that God exists, except maybe at Christmas.

But just as Aunt Anne came to be a surrogate mother for my father when relations with his own mother were strained, so God can move from our extended family to someone who makes up for the failings in our immediate circumstances. There are at least two ways to deal with the image of God as a parent when your own parent has been abusive. One is to refuse to see God in that light. So, for example, if your father continually sought your harm instead of your well-being, you might refuse to consider that father image for God since it implies all that God is not. But another way to come at that situation might be to embrace God as embodying all that fathers should be and look to God for the father experience rather than to your biological father.

That is often the role of an extended family member—to fill in when our nuclear family can't perform their god-given role, for whatever reason. In the case of Ruth and Naomi, it was a series of tragedies that brought the two women together to provide for each other as immediate family members would. The situation might be extreme, as in the case of tragedy or abuse, or it might be as simple as family members who are often unavailable due to work, illness, or emotional makeup.

In my case, my cousin Lola was the sister I never had. Although we had to sit down with complicated family charts to figure out how exactly we came to be cousins, when a brain aneurysm took her at age forty-four, it felt like I had lost a sister. On the one hand it was a huge loss. On the other hand, it was a huge gift that I had a cousin who could, at least for a while, give me the experience of sisterhood.

So as we look at our own extended families, I think it is helpful to find the voice of thanksgiving for those who have shown the face of God to us in one way or another. Even more helpful is looking out over our extended networks to ask ourselves whether there is someone out there who needs us to be God with skin on for them.

That can be a tricky business, since extended family members who are seen as interfering are a primary reason for family discord. "Yes, my daughter-in-law clearly needs me to move in and raise my grandson" may not be a universally accepted truth. There are issues of enabling, codependency, shirking of responsibility, and all sorts of possible pitfalls when it comes to making such moves. And yet the world is full of grateful praise for the Ruths and Naomis of this world.

I preached recently on the story of Abraham's wife Sarah laughing when told she would have a son in her old age. After the service someone said, "We have so many Sarahs in this congregation." She didn't mean that lots of elderly women were conceiving. She meant that lots of grandmothers were unexpectedly stepping in to raise their children. My mother's mother ran off with another man when my mother was a toddler. It was her great-grandmother who stepped in and raised my mother, living to see her married. "Grandma Card," as everyone knew her, was the rock that held an often-troubled family together over generations. She gave the gift of faith to my mother.

At least in my own life, being God with skin on for others in my extended family has happened naturally and as a matter of course. Lola and I did not decide that we would behave like sisters. It just happened. But there were things that our parents did to provide an atmosphere where that happening was possible. Our parents' sense of family dictated that cousins who lived close should be included in family activities. We went to each other's birthday parties. We saw each other Christmas Day. We had sleepovers, and our parents arranged for play dates.

The understanding of family that we had also meant that we were willing to help each other out. Lola and I lived within twenty minutes of each other, but we were in different towns. From middle school onward, I went to school in her town, which meant there was no school bus to pick me up. With both of my parents working, that presented a problem and they worked it out by delivering me to Lola's house early in the morning. I ate breakfast with her family and then Lola and I caught the bus together. Lola's mother ran a 4-H group. My parents made sure my brother and I were in it to support her. When we took a month-long camping trip across the country's national parks, we brought Lola with us.

So while the feeling of sisterhood happened naturally for Lola and me, there was an overarching family ethos that made such a natural bond possible. It is that sense of what it means to be family that either helps or hinders our ability to truly be God with skin on for those in our extended families.

Of course sometimes the ethos is not flexible and therefore is not helpful. If Lola and I were always at each other's throats and our parents forced us to be together constantly "because she's your cousin," I'm not sure I would be writing about a helpful family ethos. If you had to go visit Uncle Vinny because he was family, even though he molested you whenever you went, that would not provide an atmosphere where positive experiences of God would flourish.

And yet, despite all the potential pitfalls and all the times that such efforts go terribly wrong, person after person has a story about that special extended family member who showed them, explicitly or implicitly, the unconditional love of God. Somewhere there is the Aunt Anne, the Grandma Card, the Lola who would feel all out of sorts if you compared them to God, but who represent to us what the Bible claims is the nature of our Creator.

DISCUSSION QUESTIONS

1. If God were a member of your family circle, would God be more like nuclear family or some member of the extended family?
2. Is there an extended family member who has ever been God with skin on for you?
3. Do you think there has ever been a time when you have been God with skin on for someone in your extended family?
4. Describe the "family ethos" you grew up with as it related to extended family members. Was it helpful?

Section
2
The Outsiders

W hile our family relationships usually have the greatest influence on our lives and how we live them, they are not the only relationships we have. In a good situation, our families of origin have given us enough self-confidence, trust, and social skills to branch out and meet others. For most of us, this happens at school.

While we learned something of the nature of authority from our parents and grandparents, that authority had a different basis than that of our teachers and the principal. Ideally we obey our parents out of love. We obey our teachers because we are told we have to. Or else. Depending on how well we learn that lesson, we become exposed to many types of authority, including principals, law enforcement, and circuit court judges. We come to understand the kind of authority that is earned through exceptional knowledge and skill in a particular area and experiment with our own power over others. Eventually we apply what we have learned in the workplace, as a boss, as an employee, or both.

As we navigate the often treacherous waters of relationships across our lives, we find friends and allies. We also discover enemies who actively seek to harm us. We try to determine whether a new acquaintance is someone we can trust, someone we can work with, or someone to avoid. We become political. We become drama queens or shrinking violets, fierce competitors or "yes men." We join neighborhood associations or opt for a farm in the country. We learn how to get what we want and discover the extent and limits of our moral compass.

The family may be the predominant image for church life in American Christianity, but in the Bible it is much more complex. Jesus talks very little about "family," and what he does say in that regard is a bit shocking to those accustomed to thinking of Jesus as the "family values" guy. Instead of the family of God, the hands-down largest topic of Jesus' teaching in the Gospels is the Kingdom of God. But Americans have issues with kings, and over two hundred years later there are still those who would remove such language from our faith. I'll never forget confidently singing, "Seek ye first the kingdom of God" when I visited a congregation only to hear all those around me singing, "Seek ye first the commonwealth of God"!

Many of our denominational struggles surround issues of power and authority. One of the main reasons the British Methodist Church won't become part of the United Methodist Church is the latter's insistence that the church hierarchy include bishops. Not that some wariness is not advised. You can't pick up the newspaper without realizing that power and authority can be and are being abused in this world on a scale almost too horrible to comprehend.

My point is simply that it is not just family issues that spill over into both our personal faith and our life together in religious community. Jesus, in particular, has much more to say about these broader relationships than about our immediate families. We're to love both our neighbors and our enemies. Metaphor after metaphor shows us how the Kingdom of God is different than earthly kingdoms, and you wouldn't have much of the Hebrew Scriptures left if you tossed out all the ways God tries to teach kings to behave

*and the ways the prophets lambasted their hearers for not extend-
ing justice to those less fortunate.*

*Paul tries to pull both of those traditions together as he argues
for seeing the Church as the "Body of Christ," where we work
together for the good of the world, being "God with skin on" for
others. He spends a lot of time laying out what he thinks that looks
like for specific relationships in his specific time and culture, but
he is clear at the end of Ephesians 5 that while he may use human
examples, he is really talking about Jesus Christ and his church.*

*To a casual observer, it seems like the issue British Methodists
have with bishops may have more to do with the bitter struggles
between Protestants and Catholics in British history than it has
with theology. And maybe if the American colonies had been
given independence as a gift from George III instead of wresting it
by force, we would find fewer objections to kingdom language in
the Bible. Or maybe not. It's a hard theory to test.*

*But I think it's worth considering that the often destructive
"politics" of church life and the frequent issues that people of faith
have with a God who has the authority of a King might have more
to do with our experiences of such relationships in the flesh than
we let on. And, just maybe, if an enemy listens to the parable of the
Good Samaritan, swallows her pride and lifts me up out of a ditch,
we can travel the bridge from the Church out into the world and
fulfill the prayer, "thy kingdom come, thy will be done on earth as
it is in heaven."*

I Get By with a Little Help

Relationships with our friends

When Celeste and I realized that we had been friends for thirty years, we decided to celebrate with a mini-vacation together. When she announced the plan to her daughter, she was answered with rolled eyes and the words, "Great. Now you're going to come back sounding like Anne again."

I don't know what she meant exactly, and I am not sure I want to enquire about why "sounding like Anne" would be such a frustrating thing for the family, but it does point out a basic truth about close friends: We come to be like them.

This is not some sort of magic. In fact, studies have shown that it is intentional on our part, at least at a subconscious level. There is actually evidence that "people choose friends who are genetically similar to them, and that the similarity cannot be fully explained as due to the tendency to choose friends who look like oneself."[3]

Dr. Robert Cialdini draws on a number of psychological studies to determine the following "rules" for why we like others and how that translates into behavior. While Cialdini is most interested in how these things make us suckers for certain kinds of sales pitches, it also has implications for how we choose our friends and how those friendships develop.

To see how we come to both select our friends and become like them, consider the following "rules of liking" presented by Cialdini.

1. We most prefer to say yes to the request of someone we know and like.
2. A halo effect occurs when one positive characteristic of a person dominates the way that person is viewed by others. And the evidence is now clear that physical attractiveness is often such a characteristic.
3. We like people who are similar to us.
4. We tend, as a rule, to believe praise and to like those who provide it, oftentimes when it is clearly false.
5. We like things that are familiar to us. Our attitude toward something is influenced by the number of times we have been exposed to it in the past.
6. Although the familiarity produced by contact usually leads to greater liking, the opposite occurs if the contact carries distasteful experiences with it.
7. An innocent association with either bad things or good things will influence how people feel about us.
8. Whenever our public image is damaged, we will experience an increased desire to restore that image by trumpeting our ties to successful others. At the same time, we will most scrupulously avoid publicizing our ties to failing others.[4]

With that information, we can see why it might be true that we become like our friends. We might even seek out a friend specifically for characteristics we would like to acquire. Here's how it works: To begin with, we're most likely to begin a friendship with someone who is similar to us in some way already (#3). Then, since we also grow to like familiar things with positive associations (#5 & #6), every time we have a good time with a friend and that friend suggests we have pizza while we're doing it, we will have frequent and positive associations with pizza. Result? Pizza stock rises and our family says, "Why do we always have pizza after you and John go fishing but tacos when you fish with Mark?"

Your family also might question why you like fishing at all since you never had an interest before meeting John. But since you and John were already friends after bonding in chemistry class, when he asked you to go fishing, you found it hard to say no to a friend (#1). After several times it was a familiar activity (#5), you enjoyed John's company and thus had positive associations (#6), so you began to like fishing yourself. That made you more similar to John (#3), which deepened how much you like each other. You see how it goes.

What has that got to do with faith? While we'll draw this out more in the last section of this chapter, here's an example. The fact that we like those who are similar to us may account for why the hymn is "What a friend we have in *Jesus*," and not "What a friend we have in *God*." The humanity of Jesus makes him similar enough to consider friendship, while the otherness of God is a barrier that few can overcome. More on that later.

Of course the influence of our friends can also apply to nefarious activities as well, which is why parents become so concerned over the friends of their children. While it is possible that your child will exert a positive influence over the others, rules #2 and #8 dictate that if the friend is more attractive than your child and if your child has self-esteem issues, it is the friend and not your child that will have the influence. If the friend is also older and therefore is seen as carrying greater authority, the Milgram experiment,[5] described later in the authority chapter, should tell you that the friend will win the influence battle just about every time. For good or for ill, we become like our friends.

Of course we can also see from those "rules" how friendships fail. It may be that a friendship is never securely anchored in the first place. If the similarity that draws us together is superficial (we both prefer Italian food or like Bruce Springsteen), the friendship may not survive the attempt to deepen it. If we go to see the Boss in concert and your enthusiasm manifests in stripping off your clothes and streaking through the audience while I prefer to applaud politely, neither of us will be inclined to take the relationship further, despite our common appreciation for the music.

The same is true if a friendship is formed because of certain conditions, like working in the same office or attending the same church. As long as the condition remains, the thing we have in common keeps us together. But when you get a new job in another city, I find that we no longer have late-night sharing about our toxic boss or the lurid lifestyle of a coworker. We drift apart.

R.B. Hays in 1988 defined friendship as "voluntary interdependence between two persons over time, that is intended to facilitate social-emotional goals of the participants, and may involve varying types and degrees of companionship, intimacy, affection, and mutual assistance."[6] While I don't recommend writing that out on a card for potential friends to sign, looking at such a definition can help us figure out why a friendship either ends or never gets going in the first place. One of those reasons could be that we have confused liking with true friendship.

You may like me because I voluntarily mow your lawn every week and I may like you for saying kind things when I do. But if I assume that such liking means we're friends, it's only a matter of time before my feelings will be hurt because you can't take time to do something else together or to listen to my personal struggles. All friends like each other, but not all those who like each other are friends. Friendship is "voluntary interdependence." One-sided or manipulated friendships have an inherent flaw that, like building a house with rotted boards, will compromise the integrity of the structure.

Friendship is unique among our intimate relationships in being freely chosen throughout its duration. In most cases, we cannot choose our parents, children, siblings, or extended family. In America most of us can choose our spouse, but once that choice is made it takes a court order to unmake it. There are many close relationships with authority figures—teachers, pastors, counselors, etc.—but the power imbalance in such relationships is problematic enough that most of the relevant professional organizations forbid the development of such relationships into anything intimate. What is the basis for such restrictions? The person with the lesser power is never truly free of influence in making such a choice. The personal relationship is never really voluntary.

Church members take note. Most of us realize that sexual relations with the pastor are out of bounds, but few really understand that close friendships fall into the same category. You and your pastor may like each other very much. If you had met as colleagues you might have become best buddies. But a pastor and a parishioner can never be friends in the above definition. You depend on the pastor for many things, but if the pastor depends on you also (as is necessary in a true, interdependent friendship) that is a violation of the pastor's role and, in many cases, is considered clergy abuse.

Perhaps this dynamic is why it is only at the Last Supper, when Jesus is about to leave his disciples for good, that he can say to them, "I do not call you servants any longer, because the servant does not know what the master is doing; but I have called you friends, because I have made known to you everything that I have heard from my Father" (John 15:15).

One last thing about the nature of friendship before we get into the more detailed implications for our faith. Friendships need maintenance. The types of maintenance needed vary greatly according to the personalities and circumstances of each pair of friends. However, they generally include "sharing activities, spending time together, engaging in rewarding and effective communication, and providing support to each other."[7] The implications of technology on friendship are obvious. For those who use social networks, chat, e-mail, or even just the lowly phone, you can see how that might help keep a long-distance friendship afloat where it otherwise might fall apart.

With that theoretical background on friendships, let's look at some biblical examples.

THE BIBLICAL WITNESS

Perhaps the most famous friends in the Bible are David, who becomes King of Israel, and Jonathan, the son of King Saul. Their relationship shows the degree of intimacy that can come with friendship. In fact, their relationship has so many aspects of a romance that it has been suggested that this is a biblical example of a homosexual relationship. Whatever you think about that theory, when a relationship begins with one person stripping naked as an act of covenant love (1 Sam. 18:1–4) and ends with a forced separation where the two kiss, and weep (1 Sam. 20:41), it's hard not to imagine we're reading a biblical Romeo and Juliet.

When Jonathan sees David for the first time, after David has slain Goliath, we read: "When David had finished speaking to Saul, the soul of Jonathan was bound to the soul of David, and Jonathan loved him as his own soul" (1 Sam. 18:1). When Jonathan is killed in battle, David grieves, saying, "I am distressed for you, my brother Jonathan; greatly beloved were you to me; your love to me was wonderful, passing the love of women" (2 Sam. 1:26). Jonathan puts David's concerns above the concerns of his own father, and David swears faithfulness to Jonathan's descendants.

A troubling piece is Saul's condemnation of the relationship when Saul says to his son, "You son of a perverse, rebellious woman! Do I not know that you have chosen the son of Jesse to your own shame, and to the shame of your mother's nakedness?" (1 Sam. 20:30)

Saul's slam of Jonathan is the reason I wanted to use this controversial illustration for friendship. We can't say for sure whether this was a gay relationship or not. In the argument's favor the Bible makes no mention of Jonathan having a wife, but David is married during this period to Saul's daughter, Michal, and his lust for the lovely Bathsheba gets David in some famously hot water later on. It's an open question. But there are other types of intimacy besides sexual, and there are non-sexual forms of physical expression. Our culture seems to have a difficult time with both of those things.

I have said elsewhere that I believe American culture is too neurotic about sexuality to come to healthy conclusions about physical expression. What that means for a close friendship is that any sort of physical expression between same-sex friends will have at least one Saul looking down his nose in suspicion. Nowhere did I feel that as much as when I was a single pastor of a church. I lived alone and no matter how lonely I might become, that was my only real option. I don't believe in getting married just to have a roommate. But if a male friend moved into the parsonage, my pastoral career would have been over, even if we never so much as shook hands. If a female friend moved into the parsonage, my career would have ended even sooner, unless she were obviously disabled and in need of care.

As I began my ministry, I was keenly aware of how people would talk if I entertained male friends. So I very consciously cultivated relationships with women. Did it help? Nope. Soon the pastor-parish relations committee was getting reports that I was a lesbian. It was a no-win situation.

Celeste and I have been friends now for thirty-six years. While I don't think I would express that as David did by saying that my love for her surpasses the love of men, it is true that it has outlasted any romantic relationship I've ever had and has survived when a marriage could not. And it could be that the only reason I wouldn't describe it as surpassing the love of men or hold her hand when we walk down the street is because the Sauls of the world then would take what is beautiful and call it shameful.

The other biblical friendship that I find interesting is the friendship between Abraham and God. While the "otherness" of God might provide some stumbling blocks for human beings feeling any particular closeness, the story of Abraham at least lets us know that God does not deem friendship with human beings inappropriate. Let's look at Genesis 18.

Recognizing the principle that we like those who are similar to us, God appears to Abraham in Genesis 18:2 as three men. They have come to let Abraham know that Sarah will have a child in her old age. In earlier chapters we're told that the Lord "appeared" to Abraham, but aside from the bizarre smoking firepot that marks the covenant in Genesis 15, we're not told what form that appearance took. In Genesis 18, God appears in the flesh, and Abraham is able to interact with the men as one would with others at the beginning of a friendship. He provides hospitality.

From there we move to the story of the destruction of Sodom and Gomorrah with God still very literally embodied in the three men. Genesis 18:17 is one of the most amazing verses in all of Scripture to me. As God considers wiping out the cities, God muses, "Shall I hide from Abraham what I am about to do . . . ?" This is not just a one-way relationship. God is uncomfortable not sharing such dramatic plans with Abraham. So the men tell Abraham that the outcry from the cities has been great and they must go investigate.

In the next verses, from verse 23–33, Abraham has his famous bargaining session with God over whether God's action is truly just, since righteous people may live in the doomed cities. Although Abraham's words are punctuated with some version of "Oh do not let the Lord be angry if I speak" (v. 30), clearly Abraham feels comfortable enough with God to challenge God's decision and to keep taking the bargain up a notch.

Abraham starts with, "Suppose there are fifty righteous within the city; will you then sweep away the place and not forgive it for the fifty righteous who are in it?" (v. 24). When God agrees to that, Abraham keeps moving the bar. What if there are forty-five? How about forty? Thirty-five? Thirty? He pushes God all the way down to ten and God keeps conceding. If God's investigations turn up as few as ten righteous people in the city, God will not destroy it. Then we are told that the Lord went on his way.

Of course there are two ways to argue the question of God having an actual friendship with a man. One is that God has such a close relationship with Abraham because of Abraham's special place in salvation history. God also forges close relationships with Elijah, David, and the prophets, to name a few, but they are all men of note. However, they were men of note because of their faith. Does God enter into relationship only with "special" people or is opening up to God's friendship the test of faith which allows God to use people in special ways?

As a Christian, I think that is answered in the person of Jesus. Christians are always saying that God loved us so much that he died for us. Well, I think we should back that way up to Christmas. God loved us enough to be born for us. God enters the Sodom of earth, not to spend the night like the three men in Genesis, but to live a lifetime, trying to teach enough of earth's inhabitants to be righteous so that the city will not be destroyed.

Jesus is God's acknowledgment that most people would have difficulty forming an intimate friendship with a God who is as likely to appear as a smoking firepot as three guys under an oak tree. Most of us need God with skin on to form a friendship. We need someone who is similar to us. Jesus is God's way of saying that God would like to have a relationship with each of us like the one God had with Abraham. The chasm between God and us is wide, and God was not content that only some people could manage to cross it. God built a bridge on Christmas.

GOD WITH SKIN ON

Jesus may have been the first explicit bridge from humanity to God, but we've cut short our creed if we end it there. The purpose of the Holy Spirit is to enable the disciples to fulfill the mission Jesus describes in John 17:18 in his prayer for them: "As you have sent me into the world, so I have sent them into the world." Through the power of the Holy Spirit, the disciples of Jesus, both then and now, are empowered to be the continuing incarnation of Christ in the world. We are the Body of Christ, God with skin on.

What that means in terms of friendship is that we become the means for people to build a friendship with God. To the extent that we are faithful to the vows of our baptism, the human friendships we cultivate extend beyond ourselves and back to the God whose name we have taken upon ourselves in Christ. *So, Anne, are you saying that anybody who is friends with me is becoming a friend of God at the same time?* Yes. That's what I'm saying. Unless of course you're living like the devil, in which case they're becoming friends with Old Harry, Mr. Scratch himself.

Think back to those "rules of liking" that we talked about at the beginning of the chapter. Remember that those rules are based in psychology but come from a book that is a standard text in advertising and marketing. That guy on the car lot selling you that Honda or Ford is working those rules to get you to like him. But that's not because he wants more friends to go out with after work. It's because if you like the salesman, you will extend your fondness to the product he represents and become more likely to buy the car.

It's the same principle at work when you, who wear the nametag "Christian," develop a relationship with someone. Hopefully you're not manipulating and forming false friendships in order to "sell" Jesus. That's the stuff of cults, not true Christianity. But whether false or true, our psychological makeup dictates that as I grow to like you, I will also grow to *be* like you. I will look more favorably on the things that you value than I might otherwise, which is why word-of-mouth advertising is the best kind of advertising you can get.

As I experience your faith through your actions, it becomes more familiar to me, which makes me more inclined to like it and make it a part of my own lifestyle. One caveat is that this can work the other way if the experience is negative. If every discussion of religious matters with your friends ends up with you explaining that the fires of hell await their unregenerate souls, we are no longer in the realm of sharing pleasant experiences. Regardless of whether you are technically right or wrong, the mechanics of psychology will kick in and you will either lose the friend or religion will become off-limits as a topic of discussion.

What I want to say is that when a friend has a negative experience with your faith, due to either your actions or your words, you haven't just lost a friend or an argument. You have made it more difficult for that person to become friends with God. If the guy in the auto showroom that you liked so well gets you to buy a car and it catches fire while you are driving it home, chances are you're going to swear off the entire brand, not just that particular salesman or that particular car. The same is true with faith. It's how we're wired.

The good news is that positive experiences with our friends are the easiest forms of evangelism there are. "Love me, love my God." As long as you aren't tacking on the "or else" at the end of the sentence, that becomes almost automatic. I remember in one of the churches I served how one person coming to church turned quickly into a whole pew full of her friends and neighbors, just because the first person lived her faith with joy and love. Once the friends and neighbors had met Jesus in that woman, they found they were friends of Jesus, too. I also remember one friend of mine who had a past filled with many negative church experiences. "Religion is not for me," he said, "but I love the God I see in you." I think that counts, even if he never darkens a church door.

I truly believe that we introduce Christ to others when we introduce ourselves. Our job is to make sure that we give a true introduction and that we immediately fess up when our actions fail to be guided by our faith.

But suppose I'm the person who had the metaphorical car catch fire? Suppose I'm the one molested by the pastor, the one judged to be fit only for hell, the one betrayed by a friend who spends every Sunday in church but who stabbed me in the back without thinking twice? Can I ever hope to sing about my friendship with Jesus?

Yes, although it's hard. One of the reasons I'm laying out psychological studies and theories in these chapters is because we have a better shot at avoiding manipulation, even from our own brains, when we understand what's happening. To go back to the car analogy, it's not only true that I can be tricked into buying a lemon if I like the salesman, but I also can be dissuaded from the best car on the lot because the person trying to sell it to me is a complete jerk. When you look at the tactics of marketing it becomes pretty clear that how I feel about a product I have not yet used has almost nothing to do with the merits of the product. That's why we turn to the recommendations of our friends, to help us cut through the hype and be sure it's the car we want and not the sexy lifestyle the ad promises we'll have.

When we recognize that we are influenced in our feelings toward religion by our experiences with those who practice it, we have a better shot at finding the truth. Just because some doctors are quacks doesn't mean that there's no help to be found in medicine, and just because some Christians violate God's love doesn't mean that there is no love in God.

The problem of associating the quality of the product with the quality of the person advocating it is one of the reasons why having the experience and the stories of Jesus is so important. When God just relied on human beings to show God's love (even the amazing personages of Abraham, Moses, Elijah, and David), there were slips. Big ones. There was no perfect example of the life to which God calls us. So God came and lived it in the flesh. Jesus.

When the faith expressed in the lives of our friends leaves us cold, we can search out the truth in the Gospels. Jesus certainly wasn't always warm and fuzzy, so it's possible that the discomfort we felt with our human friend is in fact a faithful reflection. But it's also true that Jesus came down hard on religious leaders for associating God's love and mercy with things that express neither. Because a friend is religious doesn't mean their lives and opinions always reflect God's will. While it is much easier to sing "What a friend we have in Jesus" when our earthly friends have behaved toward us in Christ-like ways, sometimes we learn to sing "What a friend we have in Jesus" because he is the only friend that has been willing to love us as we are.

Ironically, when we have that experience of God's love directly from its source, we are then better prepared to live out that love in our human relationships. The one betrayed by a Christian friend who is willing to take the pain of that betrayal to the throne of grace can become a living embodiment of Christ for others in a way the betraying friend never will.

DISCUSSION QUESTIONS

1. Who was the first friend you ever had? What happened with that friendship? Why?
2. Have there been patterns in your friendships, either in the way they are formed or the way they end?
3. Have you ever felt that Jesus was your friend? How about God?
4. Describe a time when you fell for an advertising gimmick. What got you?
5. Has a bad experience with a Christian ever turned you or someone you know away from Christian faith? What was that like? Did the actions of the Christian accurately reflect the Jesus in the Gospels?
6. Have you ever been attracted to Christian faith because of a friend? How did that happen?
7. Describe the most Christ-like person you know personally. Is that person a professing Christian? Does that matter?

From Classroom
to Cubicle

Relationships with our peers

Early in my ministerial career, I was appointed to an exciting church. In my first months I was overjoyed at the reception I received, the opportunities that I was given to stretch my wings, and was just generally happy about my situation. During that first six months I went to a gathering of clergy colleagues. I beamed to everyone I met about my happiness in the new situation. At least three different people, however, responded with a warning. "You shouldn't talk about it," they all said in one way or another. "Not everyone is happy in their situations and some will be jealous and try to bring you down."

As I continued on in ministry and became known for my preaching skills, I began to encounter colleagues who confessed to me that they were not overjoyed to learn that I was being appointed to a church in their region. They feared that members of their congregations would migrate over to me, making them look somehow inferior. When I left parish ministry altogether and took the helm of the Massachusetts Bible Society, my excitement about my new job was met with snide remarks, anger, and disappointment from some colleagues who disagreed with my decision.

Such conflicts and competitive instincts enter into most of our relationships at some point or another, but I think they are especially obvious in our relationships with peers. Of course our peers might become friends or lovers or enemies, but in this chapter I want to look at the relationships we have with those we know because of some common association but who we would not consider part of an inner circle of either friends or antagonists and who are our relative equals.

That description would include coworkers who are neither our boss nor someone we supervise; colleagues who share a professional career path (clergy, doctors, foremen, teachers, administrators, etc.); people who belong to the same book group, school, Rotary Club, church, playgroup, scout troop, neighborhood. You get the idea. There are lots of those folks, and for most of us in our active years they outnumber all of our close relations combined. How do we relate to them?

We noted earlier that the patterns of behavior we learn with our brothers and sisters (the first "peers" that most of us meet) carry over into our adult relationships with others. In those early relationships, either with siblings or our first experiences in playgroups, we learn whether these mysterious "others" who appear in our world should be welcomed as helpers or viewed as potential competitors.

Let's say Naomi is having a great time on the swing in the playground and I am waiting for my turn. Initially I'm very excited that Naomi is having a great time because that means swings are fun and I'm going to have that fun next. But if Naomi is having so much fun that she won't give me my turn, I start to feel differently. Now her fun is taking away from my fun. And if she stays on the swing so long that play time is over and I have to leave without ever getting my turn, there's going to be no waiting in line the next time Naomi and I find ourselves on the playground together. I'm going to tear into the yard to try to beat her to the swing.

Further, if this is my first ever experience in playing with another child, I might well assume that the new kid who just wandered in will behave just like Naomi if he gets to the swing first. I have unconsciously learned that resources (in this case swings) are scarce, and if I want to be happy, I will have to stop just waiting my turn and compete.

Of course things might have worked out differently. Naomi might have been having so much fun on the swing that she imagined it could be twice as fun with two. Seeing me standing there, she might have invited me to sit on her lap and see if we could both swing together. Then, when we both fell off into the dirt laughing she might have said, "Here, you get on and I'll push you. Then I'll get on and you can push me." In that scene, when the new kid came into the playground, we might well have broken the swing trying to load all three of us on the same seat or we might have needed grownups to drag us away because we stayed so long taking turns pushing each other on the swing.

If *that* were my first experience with another child, I would have unconsciously learned that my happiness was enhanced by others and would likely see any new person as a potential help to me rather than as a potential threat. In those early encounters, whether with siblings or other children, I am learning about more than just Naomi and swing sets. I'm learning how to get what I need in a world where there are whole bunches of people doing the same thing, and I will carry what I learn into the rest of my life.

A study about competition in friendships that we'll look at in a minute notices, "Doing well in American culture frequently corresponds to beating someone else. This society of winners and losers avails itself of a language that mirrors these values. In a culture where one 'wins a promotion, beats the other sales clerks, outsmarts a teacher, becomes a superstar, defeats enemies, and is the best student,' a day without competition is rather unlikely. It permeates all aspects of America including the economy, education, leisure, and the workplace."[8]

It's no wonder that a competitive spirit seeps into relationships with our peers. But is that a bad thing? Doesn't competing help us become better? Doesn't it enhance our self-esteem? Well, yes, if we win. But we all know Frank, the kid who is never picked in that horrible competition of picking teams for gym class. One by one every boy in the room is selected for a team as Frank looks down and shuffles his feet. Finally, he is the only one left and the last captain, with a look of disgust, motions that Frank should come to their side. His new teammates groan.

No self-esteem boost there, and by the time the game starts Frank has been so humiliated in front of the class that he's unlikely to be able to focus enough to do well and change their opinion. In fact, he might be so upset that he trips and falls, letting the ball go to the other team and losing the game. When his teammates are then branded as "losers," they will cry bloody murder tomorrow when the gym teacher insists that he's got to go on somebody's team.

Should we compete or cooperate? Or should we do some of each depending on the circumstance? It's worth looking at in terms of what those who study competition have found and in terms of what the Bible might have to teach us on the subject. I found two studies on competition that seemed to shed some light. One is from the world of business and the other from the study of relationships.

The business study looked at the field of Formula 1 racing and how the competition between the companies who developed the engines for the racecars affected both their own bottom line and the sport as a whole. They found that when a company was highly competitive, keeping its techniques and formulas away from the prying eyes of other engine manufacturers, the company rose to the top of its class.

On the other hand, when there was a sharing of technologies, methods, and information—a more open-source approach—the result was a successful overall industry. In other words, competition produced an engine that was superior to all the others and a good bottom line for the company that made it. Cooperation produced a variety of good engines across the board and a number of firms with sustainable profits.[9]

We'll look at that through the lens of the Bible in a minute, but first let's look to the relationship study. This one was specifically looking at competition in same-sex platonic friendships and whether that helped or hindered the friends in working through conflicts. Did competing with friends help, hurt, or make no difference in these relationships? When conflict came up, did competition contribute skills that would help in resolving it? Was there a difference in what the competition was about? Was it different for men and women?

The results first showed that both men and women had competition in their friendships, even though men competed more in some categories (like sports) and women in others (like social skills). What it showed across the board, however, was that competition in all seven of the areas they looked at resulted in greater difficulty working through conflicts, thus placing more strain on the friendship.[10]

And then there was a separate investigation into competition at a boys' summer camp by social scientist Muzafer Sherif. I'll just quote the description.

> It didn't take much to bring on certain kinds of ill will. Simply separating the boys into two residence cabins was enough to stimulate a "we vs. they" feeling between the groups; and assigning names to the two groups (the Eagles and the Rattlers) accelerated the sense of rivalry. The boys soon began to demean the qualities and accomplishments of the other group. But these forms of hostility were minor compared to what occurred when the experimenters purposely introduced competitive activities into the factions' meetings with one another. Cabin against cabin treasure hunts, tugs-of-war, and athletic contests produced name-calling and physical friction. During the competitions, members of the opposing

team were labeled "cheaters," "sneaks," and "stinkers." Afterward, cabins were raided, rival banners were stolen and burned, threatening signs were posted, and lunch-room scuffles were commonplace.[11]

In order to undo the mess they had created, Sherif and the other experimenters created situations where goals could only be reached through cooperative efforts. After a series of such activities, here's what happened:

> Before long, the verbal baiting had died, the jostling in lines had ended, and the boys had begun to intermix at the meal tables. Further, when asked to list their best friends, significant numbers changed from an earlier exclusive naming of in-group chums to a listing that included boys in the other group. Some even thanked the researchers for the opportunity to rate their friends again because they realized they had changed their minds since the old days. In one revealing episode, the boys were returning from a campfire on a single bus— something that would have produced bedlam before but was now specifically requested by the boys. When the bus stopped at a refreshment stand, the boys of one group, with five dollars left in its treasury, decided to treat their former bitter adversaries to milkshakes![12]

It seems that as far as researchers are concerned, there are reasons to handle competition with caution. So, with that as background, let's look at how the Bible approaches the subject.

THE BIBLICAL WITNESS

Competition is everywhere in the Bible. Right out of the gate we have the snake pitting God against Adam and Eve in the quest for knowledge. "Eat this fruit and put yourself on a level playing field with God," he says in effect. "Even the odds. God is just trying to quash competition by forbidding you to eat." Of course we know how that turned out. The first siblings competed in their offerings to God and it resulted in the first murder.

We've already seen in detail the competitive rivalry between Jacob and Esau and saw how God turned competition on its head by throwing the wrestling match by the Jabbok River. There's the smack down between Moses and Pharaoh, Elijah and the prophets of Baal, Israel and its neighbors, kings and those who would supplant them. Things are no better as we turn to the New Testament. The disciples argue amongst themselves about who is the greatest, and the earliest Christian communities were developing a competitive my-founder-is-better-than-your-founder spirit, forcing Paul to respond, "What then is Apollos? What is Paul? Servants through whom you came to believe, as the Lord assigned to each" (1 Cor. 3:5).

Paul certainly spends a lot of ink trying to get those first churches to realize that they were not separate entities in competition with each other but rather "we, who are many, are one body in Christ, and individually we are members of one another" (Rom. 12:5). Perhaps recognizing our competitive nature, Paul tries to steer it in another direction a few verses later saying, "outdo one another in showing honor." Interestingly, back in the study of competition between friends, the category of competition that had the least detrimental effect on the friendship for both men and women was altruism—when friends tried to outdo one another in doing good for others, in showing honor.[13]

Certainly Paul uses competitive metaphors in his letters saying, "Do you not know that in a race the runners all compete, but only one receives the prize? Run in such a way that you may win it" (1 Cor. 9:24). Overall, however, it seems that Paul would at least like to redirect our competitive spirit to things that serve the Kingdom. He collects money for the poor in Jerusalem and praises the relative giving of other churches to get people to give generously. He trumpets his own righteousness compared to others but then follows his boast with, "Yet whatever gains I had, these I have come to regard as loss because of Christ. More than that, I regard everything as loss because of the surpassing value of knowing Christ Jesus my Lord" (Phil. 3:7–8a).

I think the clearest examples, however, come from the Gospels. Very early on a rivalry begins to stir in the hearts of the disciples of John the Baptist. John has been the big game in town with crowds flocking to him to be baptized in the Jordan. But then Jesus sets up shop downstream and John's disciples come to him saying, "Rabbi, the one who was with you across the Jordan, to whom you testified, here he is baptizing, and all are going to him."

John responds with incredible grace. "The friend of the bridegroom, who stands and hears him, rejoices greatly at the bridegroom's voice. For this reason my joy has been fulfilled. He must increase, but I must decrease" (John 3:29–30). John the Baptist is the one sent to prepare the way for Jesus. Many might point to his calls for repentance and baptism as the way in which he did that. I would argue that he prepared the way for Jesus by showing that, in the Kingdom of God, the rules are different. In the Kingdom, you win by losing, thus destroying the spirit of competition.

Think about it. Competition can't exist if nobody is trying to win and if nobody wants to be seen as better than somebody else. Remember the boys' camp? Even a heated rivalry washed away when the boys worked together toward a common goal. Still, however, we strive for a win-win situation, both in business and in our personal lives. Does the Bible support the desire for win-win? That's not what John the Baptist is saying. "He must increase, but I must decrease," is not win-win. John is saying that he will lose willingly and then be truly happy in the win of another. It's not about everybody winning. It's about robbing the word "win" of any meaning by being eager to lose.

That seems also to be the approach of Jesus. When the disciples argue about which of them is the greatest, Jesus presents a child and says, "for the least among all of you is the greatest" (Luke 9:48), or as the version in Mark 9:35 has it, "Whoever wants to be first must be last of all and servant of all." That's not exactly the competitive spirit.

Lest the point be lost, when Jesus gathers with his disciples in his final days, he gets up from dinner, ties a towel around his waist and washes the feet of his disciples as a servant would do. That of course upsets the apple cart, especially with Peter, who is still very certain that important people should have privileges that others do not. Jesus explains by emphasizing both his prominence and his servanthood: "You call me Teacher and Lord—and you are right, for that is what I am. So if I, your Lord and Teacher, have washed your feet, you also ought to wash one another's feet. For I have set you an example, that you also should do as I have done to you" (John 13:13–15). Jesus was not caught up in a need to win.

Just a quick word search shows that the word "win" appears in the Gospels only once. It is in Matthew 23:15 where Jesus is blasting the Pharisees for traveling far and wide to win converts and then perverting the message. By contrast, Jesus uses the word "lose" thirteen times. Paul, on the other hand, uses "win" ten times and "lose" only twice. It's not a scientific study, but I'm guessing that's why so many churches like to stick with Paul and approach the words of Jesus only with reverent caution. We do not like to lose. We would much rather "fight the good fight" (1 Tim. 1:18) and "finish my course" (Acts 20:24) than to take seriously, "If any want to become my followers, let them deny themselves and take up their cross and follow me. For those who want to save their life will lose it, and those who lose their life for my sake will find it" (Matt. 16:24–25).

It appears that Jesus does not promote competition or model it as a way of life. Since I believe that Jesus is the revelation of God—meaning that we can understand the nature of God by observing Jesus' life—the absence of competition in the life of Jesus tells me that it is also absent in God.

That makes sense to me. We do not have to compete for God's affection. God does not prefer winners and condemn losers. The picture Jesus gives us of God's MO is that our salvation is a cooperative effort. God ties a towel around his waist and serves human beings, encouraging us to do that for each other. Instead of racing each other to the finish line, we link arms and move in fits and starts toward the goal, stopping every time someone falls behind to help them back on the road. And when all of us come upon a chasm that not even the most agile of us can jump, God lies down across the breach so that we can move on. Love is not about who wins.

GOD WITH SKIN ON

When we live our lives competitively, it is easy to carry that worldview across to our faith. If salvation is a competition, some must win and others must lose. If God loves the winners, then we must hide our sins deep rather than bringing them to the surface in repentance. If God is competitive then it is right to pray that we win the war or even the football game. If God loves the winners and condemns the losers, then so must we.

But if God keeps messing up competition by throwing the game—becoming a servant even though he could be a king, dying on a cross instead of conquering Rome, saying that the wealthy ones are those who give everything away—then our worldview looks a bit different. What if Kingdom life is about cooperation rather than competition?

If that's the case, God is not smiling when we push out our chest and run through that finish line ribbon. God might just wipe the grin off our faces, turn us around, and send us back six miles to help the one with a pulled hamstring. God might not be pleased that we never missed a Sunday in church if we used our weekly attendance to smugly put down those who only came on Christmas and Easter. We might get to the pearly gates far ahead of the pack, only to find that no one is allowed in alone.

Being God with skin on for our peers means putting aside our competitive instincts to be sure that everyone succeeds. Keeping the proprietary information will enhance us personally, but in the Kingdom, those who are first get sent to the back of the line. If you're smarter than your classmates, help them study for the tough exam. If you can see a solution to your competitor's problem, offer it. The Formula 1 racing study shows that while your own company may not be as far out in front, the larger business community will thrive. And isn't it better for all of us if there are many companies adding jobs and contributing to the GDP?

When another mom in the playgroup has a child who is slow to learn, maybe proving the superiority of your child is not the answer. Maybe you can help her find some resources and maybe she can help you learn humility. If we are responsible for structuring activities for children or youth, how might the dynamics change if those activities encouraged cooperation rather than competition? Dr. Robert Cialdini makes the case that the reason the racial integration of schools has increased racial tensions rather than alleviating them is because school is an extremely competitive environment.[14]

As Christians, our lives are supposed to be a witness to God's nature. In professing that Jesus is our "Lord," we are saying that our actions reflect his rule and his preferences for how life should be lived. I'll grant you that's a tall order, but that's why I generally have issues with altar calls. Accepting Jesus as Lord is not something to be done in the emotion of the moment. It's a decision to completely alter our lives and priorities, and those who profess it without making such changes leave Christians open to the all-too-accurate charge of hypocrisy.

Jesus makes it quite plain that being his disciple means living very differently from the world. In this case, it means giving up on entering the "rat race," the competition with others for life's toys and resources. There is no drive to keep up with the Joneses in Kingdom life. Like Paul in Philippians 4:12, we learn to be content with what we have. We don't seek to be proven better than others in competition. We take whatever gifts we have been given, tie them around our waists, and use them to serve others.

In our churches, it means that we are not in competition with the church down the street or with the other service in our own church on Sunday morning. When they grow, we rejoice because more people are finding their way to faith. We support their ham and bean supper, even if they never cross the threshold of our church fair. In our own congregations it means recognizing that even though you've been given the baritone solo in the Christmas Cantata every year for fifteen years, the new guy with the amazing voice really does deserve to have it. "He must increase, I must decrease," must become something we are capable of saying in recognition of the gifts of others.

In doing so, however, we can't let ourselves fall back into thinking that we have "lost" and are therefore less in God's eyes. God is incapable of seeing either a winner or loser. As Paul says in Galatians, "We are all one in Christ Jesus." In Paul's metaphor we are one body with many members. It's not about whether the right eye is better than the left leg. It's about whether they are each healthy and doing what they are gifted to do. Personally, I think there are few things a church can do to eliminate a spirit of competition more than engaging everyone in discovering their own spiritual gifts and then working to deploy them in ministry.

To be God with skin on for our peers means helping them to see themselves as God sees them. They are not losers. They are not winners. God is not interested in where they stand relative to anybody else. God merely wants them to wake up to their role in the body and fulfill that function to the best of their ability.

The studies show that if we take even seemingly innocent competition out of our relationships, we will have a more healthy response to conflicts. We won't get as much personal recognition as we might otherwise receive, but industry-wide, the human industry will thrive. By elevating the concept of losing, Jesus threw the game. He refused to compete and, in doing so, saved us. "For I have set you an example," Jesus said after washing their feet, "that you also should do as I have done to you."

DISCUSSION QUESTIONS

1. On a scale of 1–10, how competitive are you?
2. Remember a time when you won a competition. How did you feel? Remember a time when you lost a competition. How did you feel?
3. Did your family of origin encourage competition or cooperation? How did that happen?
4. Describe a peer relationship in which you felt a sense of competition. Did it have any impact on the relationship?
5. Have you ever seen competition in your faith community? Over what?
6. What are the benefits and drawbacks of competition?
7. What are the benefits and drawbacks of cooperation?
8. Is there a place in your life where you could turn a competition into a cooperative effort?

Yes Sir!

Relationships with authority figures

From the minute we learned that oh-so-empowering word, "no," we have been developing views about authority. With experiences from parents to school to work to the over-arching authority of government, few of us reach adulthood without "authority issues" of one sort or another. We transfer our expectations to new situations and apply both the conscious and unconscious lessons we have learned about authority to anyone with authority over us or to ourselves when we are at the top of the ladder.

You can't have authority without some sort of hierarchical system, either formal or informal. That might be the highly fluid system of the family, the dynamic structure of a business, the hierarchy of a religious group, or the detailed laws and directives of a nation. It might be implicit or explicit. We might have a say in the structure or we may not. In my house, the hierarchy is designed and run by the cat, reminding us that systems of hierarchy are not unique to human relationships. All of which means that if we are going to live in this world, we will be dealing with authority in many ways and on many levels.

We will all live under the authority of others and many of us will have authority over others at some point. Most of us are ill prepared for this.

In the 1960s, social psychologist Stanley Milgram conducted a now-infamous study on authority and obedience.[15] Ostensibly to study the effects of punishment on learning, forty volunteer subjects were asked to help a "learner" master a list of word pairs. When a mistake was made, the "teacher" was to administer an electric shock to the "learner," who was in another room. The shock level was to increase with successive mistakes, with the top level of electric shock being a truly dangerous level.

Of course since the "learner" was really a Milgram accomplice, no harm was actually done, but it remains a disquieting fact that two-thirds of the "teachers" did administer the highest level of shock, despite the accomplice's cries of distress in the other room that led the "teachers" to believe that he was suffering great pain and distress.

Even more disturbing was the Stanford prison experiment, conducted in 1971 by psychologist Philip Zimbardo,[16] to study the effects of becoming a prisoner or prison guard. Volunteers were screened for emotional health and stability. That didn't help. By just the second day there was a "prisoner" revolt and the "guards" put it down with fire extinguishers. The experiment was supposed to last two weeks. It was terminated after six days, as the treatment of the "prisoners" became so sadistic and humiliating that many subjects showed severe emotional disturbances. Unlike in the Milgram experiment, real harm was being done. While the conditions of the experiment would not pass today's ethical standards, it remains a troubling picture of how easy it is for authority to be tragically misused.

Of course I come to this with my own authority baggage. I suspect that I am not the only woman for whom "authority issues" are more frequently about failing to claim proper authority than abusing the authority we have been given. When I did a Google search on "women and authority," six out of the first ten hits were about the role of women in religious faith. At my ordination the bishop laid his hands on my head and said, "Take thou authority." In my experience as a clergywoman, that was truer than he knew. Every step of the way I have had to "take" whatever authority I could. It was almost never granted otherwise.

Whether you are a woman in a traditionally male job, the child of an alcoholic, a prison guard, a circuit judge, a parent, or a third-grade teacher, you have no doubt seen both the upside and downside of the use of authority. In my own life, the best models of authority I had were my teachers. With very few exceptions, every teacher I had from kindergarten through graduate school used authority wisely and well, and many of them I count as friends and mentors today.

The worst models I had were generally my bosses in employment. In those cases the opposite was true, with very few bosses providing a respectable balance of support, freedom, and accountability to me and to others. As a result, I am a much better teacher than I am a boss.

While the topic of authority could fill any number of books, and "authority issues" fill any number of therapy couches, what interests me is the way that our perceptions of authority color our faith and our experience of God. After all, it's hard to find a bigger authority figure than God. It sort of goes with the territory— almighty, omnipotent, no other gods before me, etc.

Even though we may say of an authoritarian boss, "He thinks he's God," thereby acknowledging God's superior status, the reality is that there are many times when we don't think even God should have quite the authority that is claimed in our creeds and doctrines. I wish someone would do a study to back this up, but my theory is that the larger "authority issues" loom in our personal relationships, the more uncomfortable we are with a God who has ultimate and unchallenged control.

For myself, I think that uncomfortable truth is part of the Good News. When the writer of Proverbs says, "the fear of the Lord is the beginning of wisdom" (Proverbs 1:7), I think he means that we begin to wake up to spiritual reality when we reach the disturbing realization that we are not in ultimate control of the world. There is an ultimate authority beyond ourselves, beyond our teachers, beyond our governments and law enforcement agents. We don't vote on that, and that authority will not be deposed by any coup d'état, insurgency, or aerial assault. Scary thought (thus the fear), but the beginning of a spiritual enlightenment.

Looking at other parts of Scripture, however, I would say that such a fearful beginning to wisdom is not its ultimate end. The first letter of John spells that out by saying that "perfect love casts out all fear" (1 John 4:18). That perfect love is the "end" of wisdom. What happens in between the beginning (fear) and the end (love) is the stuff of authority issues. Who is this God, how does God wield all that power and authority, and should I be worried? It is also the stuff of Scripture.

THE BIBLICAL WITNESS

It is as hard to escape the issue of authority in Scripture as it is in life, which shouldn't be surprising. Even in the first commune, established by the disciples in Acts 4:32–37, we see that there is still a strong hierarchy, with the apostles running the place and deciding how to distribute their common wealth. In the stories of the Bible we see all kinds of human authority, some wielded with grace and mercy, some with harsh brutality. Some authority is derived from lineage, some from wisdom, some from moral standing, some from life experience. Some is competent, some is uninformed, some is earned, some is stolen. It is just like life.

There are also teachings about authority, most notably in the New Testament. In Romans 13:1, Paul famously says, "Let every person be subject to the governing authorities; for there is no authority except from God, and those authorities that exist have been instituted by God." Peter makes obedience to authority a key theme for his entire first letter. Peter not only confirms Paul's thought that human governmental authority is to be obeyed, but also expands that to instruct slaves to be obedient to masters, even harsh ones, wives to be obedient to husbands, and so on.

The irony, of course, is that by the time Peter writes a second letter, he is writing from prison. Paul, too, ends up in prison, where both are finally executed. Both of them went to prison because they chose to disobey the governing authorities. So, no matter what a literal rendering of their instructions might imply, their lives show a belief that disobedience, at least to human authority, has a place in the life of the Christian.

Peter gives a counter-balance to his later writing in Acts 5. Peter, along with the other apostles, has been arrested for preaching in Jesus' name, which had been forbidden. An angel lets them out in Acts 5:19 and they go right back to their preaching. The authorities haul them in again and say, "We gave you strict orders not to teach in this name, yet here you have filled Jerusalem with your teaching." Peter answers, "We must obey God rather than any human authority" (Acts 5:28–29).

Paul, also, does not take "no" for an answer when it comes to doing what God has called him to do, and the authorities are on his tail for most of the book of Acts. The book of Philemon shows that Paul has been harboring an escaped slave named Onesimus. Paul does send him back to his master, but uses his own authority to be sure that Onesimus will be freed when he gets back. Alrighty then. Whatever the dictates of Romans 13 and 1 Peter might sound like, we see in the lives of both Peter and Paul that they didn't mean in those letters that we should be obedient against our own conscience, whether that conscience said to disobey the government or to free a slave.

We see the same tensions in the life of Jesus. In general, he encouraged obedience, even though Palestine was run by the Roman occupying force. He famously told his disciples that if a

Roman soldier forced one of them to carry his pack for a mile, they should do one better and go with him two. If their cloak was demanded, they should throw in their shirt as well.

In an odd sort of way, such action both is obedient to and subversive of authority. The person does what is asked and is therefore obedient, but by choosing to go beyond what is asked, the person reclaims his or her own power of choice, elevating the person in a way that the command to go a mile had tried to eliminate.

There are many, many authority-based relationships in the Bible, but perhaps the most nuanced and complex is the relationship between David and King Saul. To get the full picture, you need to read most of the book of 1 Samuel, but it is in chapter 24 that we see just how complex the emotions are underneath.

If you know nothing else about the David stories, chances are you know about David and Goliath, the shepherd boy who slays the well-armed giant with a sling and a stone. Goliath was the champion of the Philistine army, which Israel had been fighting for some time. Saul is king at the time, is witness to David's heroics, and not long after David finds himself out of his father's house and playing the harp in the court of King Saul. Chapter 16:21 tells us that Saul loved David greatly and made him his armor-bearer.

It's hard to follow the trajectory exactly, since the chronology of the text is messy, but the relationship between David and Saul is both close and rocky. We don't know what the age difference was, but David becomes best friends with Saul's son, Jonathan, indicating that Saul was a generation, at least, older. When we get to chapter 24, we'll see that David calls Saul "my father" (24:11), and Saul responds, "Is this your voice, my son David?" (24:16). Although there is no biological relation, there is a father/son dynamic going on between them.

But it's not the sort of "Come on, son, let's go fishing" relationship that a young man might hope for with his dad. Saul has been an abusive father to David. David was brought in to play the harp for Saul because Saul was mentally unstable (or had a demon—pick your theology) and the harp calmed him down. But even so, we have the story in 1 Samuel 19:10 where David is playing his harp and Saul tries to pin David to the wall with a spear. He could have just said he didn't like the music!

Saul turns on David because he has come to regard David as a rival and a threat, and that is not unfounded. Although kept a secret from Saul, Samuel has anointed David as king, a rather brash thing to do when someone else is still on the throne with no plans of leaving.

Adding insult to injury, David's early talent with slingshots turns into superior military leadership and strategy skills that earn him so much fame in battle that the women greeted his return with the chant, "Saul has killed his thousands, and David his ten thousands" (18:7). It's not surprising that the following verse reports, "Saul was very angry, for this saying displeased him." It's never good to upstage the king, and Saul begins to look more earnestly for a way to kill David.

In all of this, the characters of the two men begin to emerge. When Saul saw a rising star in his court, he had options. He could have been a real teacher and mentor to David, sharing all he knew and then pointing him to someone who could take him still further. The best teachers are willing, and even hopeful, that students will grow beyond them. Jesus shows this characteristic when he makes the amazing statement to his disciples that they and other believers "will do greater works than these, because I am going to the Father" (John 14:12). John the Baptist shows it when he says of Jesus, "He must increase, but I must decrease" (John 3:30). But such humility was beyond Saul. Instead of helping David develop his obvious gifts, Saul chose to be a rival and looked for every opportunity to stamp out the competition.

David, by comparison, shows why God chose him not only as king, but also as the king who would be the ancestor of Jesus, who would be known as "the son of David." David also had options. When Saul threw that spear and it became evident that he truly meant David harm, David could have taken at least three different paths.

He could have taken up the gauntlet that was thrown down and posed a direct challenge to Saul. He knew already that God had anointed him king and that God intended to take the kingship away from Saul. He had proven his superior skills. He had the support of the people. David could have challenged Saul for the throne right then and there and probably won. He didn't.

David could also have put God's calling and his gifts aside in order to appease Saul. He could have groveled before Saul, brown-nosing his way back into favor, and taken whatever abuse Saul decided to dish out for the sake of keeping Saul happy. He did love Saul, after all, for all his failings. Saul would probably have killed David, but he would have gone down in history as a loyal servant of the king whom he loved.

But David didn't do that either. Instead he chose a third way, a way much more nuanced and complicated. First, he protects himself. He stages one final test to be sure that Saul really is intent on killing him and when that proves to be the case, he flees to the wilderness. Others who are loyal to David find him there and he ends up with his own little army out in the desert, trying to figure out what to do as Saul tries to hunt him down.

To the men with David, the answer is obvious. Catch and kill Saul before he catches and kills David. But David will have none of it. Even beyond David's love of Saul as a father figure is the knowledge that Saul, like David, is God's anointed. Samuel anointed Saul as king at God's request, and time and time again David repeats that he will not lift his hand against the Lord's anointed.

The seriousness of this commitment is shown in the climatic scene in 1 Samuel 24. King Saul, hot on the heels of David and his men, pauses for a minute for a potty break in a nearby cave. Well, that cave just happens to be where David and his men are hiding. But they are far in the back. They can see Saul, but Saul doesn't know they're there. Saul is vulnerable and David's men taste victory.

To their dismay, however, David won't do the deed. Saul has all but handed David his head on a platter and David won't take it. Instead, David sneaks over to where Saul had placed his cloak, cuts off a corner, and then goes back to hide until Saul leaves the cave.

Then, once Saul leaves the cave, David runs out and calls to him. What does he call him? "Hey, sucker?" "Over here, you idiot?" No. "My lord the king!" he cries. His point in taking the sampling from his cloak is to prove that he is not a traitor. That he could have killed Saul but didn't. And won't. David also explains why: "This very day your eyes have seen how the Lord gave you into my hand in the cave; and some urged me to kill you, but I spared you. I said, 'I will not raise my hand against my lord; for he is the Lord's anointed'" (24:10).

Saul responds well, calling David "my son" as we noted earlier and notes, "For who has ever found an enemy, and sent the enemy safely away? So may the Lord reward you with good for what you have done to me this day" (24:19). Saul says that David is more righteous than he is and recognizes that David will indeed be king. Saul even has the audacity to ask David for a favor: "Swear to me therefore by the Lord that you will not cut off my descendants after me, and that you will not wipe out my name from my father's house" (24:21). David does so.

But they don't go skipping back to Jerusalem together. Saul goes home and David goes back to his stronghold. He knows better. Sure enough, Saul tries again to kill David and in chapter 26 David has another opportunity to kill Saul and doesn't. This time he sneaks up on a sleeping Saul and takes his spear. A similar scene ensues. "Is this your voice, my son David?" "It is my voice, my lord, O king" (26:17). Again David explains while calling one of Saul's servants to retrieve the spear, "I would not raise my hand against the Lord's anointed" (26:23).

Saul finally dies in a battle with the Philistines, who kill his son (and David's best friend) Jonathan, and Saul either takes his own life (1 Sam. 31:4) or has a servant kill him (2 Sam. 1:10). David writes a song of lament to commemorate their deaths. Then, at last, David is made king.

GOD WITH SKIN ON

When we look at authority in the Bible with broad strokes, we can see some general themes that are consistent in both the Old and the New Testaments. The first point of agreement seems to be that authority, as a concept, is a good thing that is ordained by God. Whatever abuses of authority might exist, it does not appear to be God's intention to eliminate all hierarchy, either in this life or the life to come. Biblical images of heaven are full of joy, peace, and harmony but they are not egalitarian. There aren't scenes of heaven's latest arrivals trying on God's throne for size. There is, however, the sharing of power and authority, as some of God's people are depicted as being heavenly judges, even over angels.

Now you can argue that the biblical depictions of heaven are based on the earthly experience and expectations of the writers. That may be true. But it is also true that the hierarchy of heaven that we see in the Bible is mirrored in biblical teaching about life on earth and in the way God's people have lived faithfully over millennia. If you want to claim that all forms of authority are part of our sinful nature, there's a lot of Bible to explain away.

When a Roman officer asks for healing for his servant and says to Jesus, "Lord, I am not worthy to have you come under my roof; but only speak the word, and my servant will be healed. For I also am a man under authority, with soldiers under me; and I say to one, 'Go' and he goes, and to another, 'Come,' and he comes, and to my slave, 'Do this,' and the slave does it" (Matt. 8:8–9). Jesus responds with amazement saying, "Truly I tell you, in no one in Israel have I found such faith" (Matt. 8:10).

Acknowledging and trusting in the authority of Jesus is praised by Jesus as a sign of great faith. And in that little episode is a picture of how authority is rightly used. The man has a servant, but he cares for him and is seeking his healing. He trusts that Jesus will accomplish what he says because he himself is most likely good to his word. The centurion recognizes both the effects of his own commands on others and the fact that even as an officer he is under authority as well. Here is a man who takes care of those under his authority and who approaches those with authority beyond his with humility.

That Roman centurion is God with skin on for those in his service. That is, the care that the centurion's servant experiences from his master is a mirror of God's care. I would bet that the centurion also had good examples of authority above him, allowing him to approach a new and strange authority in Jesus with hope and faith rather than with suspicion.

I have found positive experiences of authority to be as welcome as anything could be. How great a difference between the boss who makes you suffer for her mistakes and the boss who takes the rap herself. When an unruly guest finds his way into the party, what a blessing when the host deals with it directly instead of expecting the guests to find a way to cope. I currently have a wonderful employee who, when confronted with a problem facing the organization, can be heard to say with a lilt to his voice, "I don't know. Solving that is beyond my pay grade!" There is often considerable relief at not being the one with certain authority. There are also few things more maddening than having authority that others refuse to recognize or trust. Ask any substitute high school teacher.

Being God with skin on in authority relationships means helping others to appreciate the purpose and benefits of authority. It means respecting the authority of others unless such obedience violates the love of God, neighbor, and self, the law that Jesus puts above all others (Mark 12:30–31). As I learn to trust the authority of others, even when I can't clearly see the reason for what I've been asked to do, I am learning how to respond in faith when God asks something of me that I don't quite understand. When I use the authority I've been given with wisdom and humility, I am helping others learn to trust authority enough that they might be willing to someday put such trust in God.

Even Peter and Paul, who believed that all human authority was God-given, found times when their conscience demanded that they disobey someone with authority over them. Yet, both of them also spent a considerable amount of ink trying to describe how a healthy system of authority should work. While we might quibble about whether the particular social system of the first century is still appropriate today, their general plea for those in authority to act with humility and justice and for those under authority to obey is valid. It is the attitude that would eventually allow those two men to go to an unjust execution with the trust that the ultimate authority of God would find them worthy, even as their non-violent civil disobedience made a statement about the failings of such authority to reflect the justice and mercy of God.

Whether we have authority over armies or just over the dog, being God with skin on requires that we exercise that authority according to God's values: to do justice, to love mercy, and to walk humbly with God (Micah 6:8). And when we find ourselves under the authority of others, whether our boss, our religious leader, or the laws of our nation, being God with skin on requires that we give our obedience unless asked to violate the Great Commandment.

Through just and merciful leadership we bear witness to how authority is exercised in God's kingdom. Through obedience we testify that God is worthy of our trust. Through non-violent disobedience to a command that would violate God's love, we proclaim our allegiance to the authority on which all other authority is based. In becoming God with skin on in relationships of authority, we draw the distinction between the way authority on earth is too frequently applied and the way authority in heaven can be experienced.

DISCUSSION QUESTIONS

1. When have you been in a position of authority over others? Was it comfortable or uncomfortable?
2. Describe a negative experience of being under authority. Describe a positive experience of being under authority.
3. What sort of authority does/should God have in our lives?
4. Does the phrase "the Kingdom of God" bother you? Why or why not?
4. Are you struggling with an authority issue right now? Do any of these biblical passages help you in finding an answer?
5. Do you think that all authority is given by God as Peter and Paul claim?

The Devil
with Skin On

Relationships with our enemies

There are scores of people of all types who we simply don't like. They might be close family members or complete strangers, but for reasons both understandable and seemingly irrational, we have decided that we don't like them. Sometimes we don't like particular individuals, sometimes we dislike people in a particular demographic group or people who hold certain values. We dislike people for reasons that are personal, political, religious, behavioral, racial, and much more.

There are also various levels of dislike. There are people who simply annoy us, like the coworker who talks too much, the relative who has to give a bear hug even when it is unwanted, or the public figure who we hate to see given positive coverage. Then there are those people we dislike at a level that it affects our behavior. We turn down the dinner invitation, we walk the dog down a different street, we bring that person's perceived misdeeds to light in gossip, we confront them in anger, we either yell at the TV or change the channel.

Our level of dislike escalates from there to stronger behavioral responses. I might not only seek to avoid a person; I might adamantly refuse to have anything to do with them or might purposefully pick fights. I might begin to demand that my friends also dislike people at this level and sometimes give up friends who insist on being cordial with or supporting those I deem unacceptable. And, of course, when behaviors escalate to a point where we feel either a real or perceived threat from another person or group, we begin to use the language of "enemy."[17] The more we fear that another person or group might do us actual harm, the more of an "enemy" that person becomes.

The dangerous thing is that such fears are all too easily manipulated. To avoid a political rant on American politics in the 2008 cauldron in which I write this, I'll look way back to the book of Exodus and the biblical history of how the Hebrew people, who first came to Egypt as honored guests, became slaves. In Exodus 1:9–10, the king of Egypt says to his people, "Look, the Israelite people are more numerous and more powerful than we. Come, let us deal shrewdly with them, or they will increase and, in the event of war, join our enemies and fight against us and escape from the land."

There's absolutely no biblical evidence before this that the Israelites felt any sort of animosity toward the Egyptians. Why would they? They had been welcomed as immigrants when their own land suffered famine and had been treated so well that they had stayed and prospered. We don't know whether the king feared for his own rule because his people were now in a minority or if he just wanted the perceived economic advantage of slaves, but he manipulates the fear of the people by pointing out not only that the Israelites are now in the majority, but by saying that "in the event of war" they will "join our enemies and fight against us." Says who? The king is manipulating the fears of the people.

In the insightful volume *Enemy Images in American History*, the authors point out that "Enmity is usually based on some concrete facts that permit the enemy image to appear as plausible and real."[18] The Egyptian king does exactly that. The Hebrew people are reaching a majority. Studies in both humans and apes have shown that at our most instinctual levels we have an aggressive response to the intrusion of strangers into our group.[19] Expand that to a racially different group expanding out of minority status into the "space" of the previous majority and you have the setting for Egypt's fear.

Now mix in a bit of Egyptian history. The biblical dating of these events is tenuous at best, with conservative scholars placing the date of the slaves departing Egypt under Moses at about 1500 BC and more liberal scholars putting the date later, at around 1200 BC. We're told the Hebrews were slaves in Egypt for four hundred years, putting the king's supposed remarks anywhere from about 1900–1600 BC, the middle of Egypt's Middle Kingdom.

The Middle Kingdom years were a prosperous period when Upper and Lower Egypt were united after a fractious earlier time when two dynasties competed for power. Looking at the dating question from the standpoint of political and psychological analyses, you could make an argument for an earlier date for the Exodus. Consider these additional insights from *Enemy Images*:

1. Social strain of all varieties seems to be the reason why people succumb so easily to hate propaganda.[20]
2. Nativism has been most successful in periods of economic depression.
3. The image of an external enemy can help to legitimize the power structure of a state and enforce the loyalty of its citizens.[21]

So, if you are King Mentuhotep II, having just won that prior dynastic battle and established your capital at Thebes, and if you are trying to unite those factions to usher in a new age of prosperity, how do you get everybody together? Well, a common enemy sure is handy, according to insight #3 above. And if the memory of the prior age's difficulties is still fresh in the minds of the people, the social strain will still be such that manipulating them to hate the Hebrews shouldn't be too difficult. In any case, it worked in ancient Egypt, just as it has worked for millennia since. The Hebrews were enslaved and became the image of an enemy that must be thwarted at all costs.

Of course, once you move from such fears into abusive action, be it the enslavement of a people or war, you start to see actions that truly do justify the status of enemy. Atrocities are committed, harm is done, and it becomes extraordinarily difficult to find a way to peace.

That's a look at enemies on a national scale, but it really is no different with individuals. As *Enemy Images* also points out, "The only major difference between private marital 'wars' and interstate enemy images is that nations are armed and legitimized by everything that state power and legitimacy has to offer: laws, parliament, approval of the churches, unions, associations, corporations."[22]

Even in those examples of state legitimacy, however, there is a strong individual component. Groups and organizations can't hate, although hateful individuals can magnify their feelings and contribute to a mob mentality in a group. Individuals act like leaven in the dough and, according to the principles of liking that we looked at in "I Get By with a Little Help from My Friends," can influence the policies and attitudes of the groups to which they belong. But the groups, per se, do not hate and could, with the right conditioning and circumstances, release their hateful norms. It was to that work that Jesus was born and it is that work that we, as the Body of Christ, are called to continue.

THE BIBLICAL WITNESS

Although the time of Jesus is ancient history to us today, the Israelite culture was already ancient at the time of his birth. There were enemies and animosities that had been established for a millennium or more as well as newer difficulties, like the occupation of Palestine by Rome. Many of those difficulties were political, but not all. There was a racial and religious hatred of the Samaritans and the cultural exclusion of the Gentiles as well as the shunning of the lepers and others deemed "unclean."

It was in the context of such turmoil that Jesus uttered the words, "You have heard that it was said, 'You shall love your neighbor and hate your enemy.' But I say to you, Love your enemies and pray for those who persecute you" (Matt. 5:43–44). Today such statements earn you the title of idealistic fool if you are a minor player, or they get you killed if your words start to gain traction in society. Reference Jesus, Gandhi, Martin Luther King, Jr.

Consider this finding from *Enemy Images*:

> A double-standard of values is deliberately created—one for the citizens, one for the enemy. All citizens can be forced to take sides, to identify themselves with a certain enemy perception, or face the alternative of being stigmatized as saboteurs and traitors of the fatherland. Doubts and ambivalence are no longer tolerated. Enemy images are therefore the most powerful instrument for enforcing internal consensus and disciplining a society.[23]

Jesus' teaching to love our enemies is not fluff. It is treason. Jesus' statement also makes it plain that the status of "enemy" is a real one. He didn't say, "Don't have enemies." He told us what to do when we found ourselves with one. Sometimes Christians can be deluded into thinking that having enemies is somehow a sign of imperfect faith—that being Christian and having enemies should, ideally, be incompatible. Well, Jesus was perfect. And he wasn't crucified by his friends. Jesus had enemies. The apostles had enemies. We will, too. Of course our behavior might sometimes cause us to have more enemies than we otherwise might have. If your enemies outnumber your friends, you might want to examine your behavior a bit more closely. But the mere existence of an enemy doesn't mean that we have sinned or that our faith is lacking.

Sometimes, in fact, we don't even know we have an enemy until it's too late. I will never forget what I thought was a simple, sixth-grade lunch. I was just arriving at a table in the cafeteria and pulled out a chair to sit down. In one of the most obvious pieces of stagecraft I have seen either before or since, another girl dashed over from another table, made a sort of backwards leap, leading with her rump for my chair, and in true drama queen fashion fell to the floor. She then leapt up, horribly indignant, to proclaim to the entire lunchroom that I had pulled a chair out from under her.

It was just the first of a number of such stunts, the motives behind which baffle me to this day. Clearly she felt that I was her enemy—that I presented some sort of threat to her—but I never gained the slightest hint as to why and didn't know the feelings existed until the day of that flying backside in the lunchroom.

That event and my subsequent attempts to explain to the girl that I truly had not noticed that she was attempting to sit in that chair and meant her no harm were all I could think about when I read the finding: "[Perceptions of the enemy] are in their essence subjective and deeply rooted in the prerational realm. For this reason, we must from the start be prepared to accept that purely explanatory appeals for more empathy will not reach the real roots of concepts of the enemy and have little chance of success."[24] In other words, rational explanations don't affect irrational behavior and perceptions. We need other tools.

Jesus knew this, which is why we don't have lots of accounts of Jesus sitting down with the Pharisees trying to explain why they shouldn't feel threatened by him and perhaps why he remains silent before his accusers at his trial. Neither does Jesus spend a lot of time explaining the ins and outs of loving the enemy to his disciples. Instead of appealing to the intellect, Jesus does two things. He tells stories about it, and he lives it, which is what I want to look at next.

You can argue that the Jews of Jesus' day were enemies of Rome. After all, Rome was occupying their country and historians tell us that the massacre of all the babies under two years of age in Bethlehem that we read about in Matthew 2:16–18 was par for the course for King Herod. But still, the Jews and the Romans governed together, lived together, and at times even found mutual regard as we see in Luke 7 in the description of Jews pleading with Jesus to help a Roman centurion.

The true examples of an enemy in the Gospels are not so much with the Jews and the Romans but with the Jews and the Samaritans. The history of the Samaritans differs depending on who you ask, but the beginnings of the split are traced in both cases to the time of the Babylonian Exile and return in the sixth century BC.

Remember that after the reign of Solomon, Israel was divided into northern and southern kingdoms, much as Egypt had been so many millennia before. The northern kingdom was the first to fall to a foreign invader, when Assyria took over the area back in the eighth century BC. That loss wiped out ten of Israel's twelve tribes. The Samaritans claim to be a remnant of the tribe of Joseph's sons, Ephraim and Manasseh, who stayed in the land. The Jews of the southern kingdom, who didn't get conquered until a couple of centuries later, claimed that the Samaritans were a sort of mixed breed of northern kingdom tribes and Assyrians who occupied the land.

When a remnant of the southern kingdom tribes return to Jerusalem to rebuild after their exile to Babylon, the Samaritans (who had already been back in that northern area for some time) volunteered to help (Ezra 4:1–5). Their help was spurned and things got worse from there.

By Jesus' day the hatred was so entrenched that Jews would not set foot on Samaritan soil, even though the land of the Samaritans sat smack dab in the middle of Palestine. In today's geography it is basically the area of the West Bank. When Jews wanted to go from north to south or vice versa, they went way out of their way, crossing the Jordan River to the desert and walking until they could cross back again without crossing any border into Samaria. The Samaritans and Jews hated each other on both racial and religious grounds, since the Samaritans had set up their own temple on Mt. Gerazim. Josephus even mentions that the Samaritan temple had a statue to Zeus in it, which, of course, would not sit well with the Jews.

Nowhere in the Gospels do we see Jesus giving lectures about how to treat this long-standing enemy. Instead, he tells a story and he pays a visit. The parable of the Good Samaritan in Luke 10:25–37 is one of the best known. A man, presumably a Jew, is traveling the steep and dangerous road between Jerusalem and Jericho. He gets mugged and is left for dead at the side of the road. Two members of the Jewish ruling class, a priest and a Levite, come along, see the man, and walk on by. A Samaritan comes along, has pity on the man, and helps him well beyond the call of duty.

This is a politically incorrect story. To make the two who fail to help very specifically part of the religious leadership and then make the hero someone that those leaders would consider an enemy would not have been received as a warm and fuzzy story in Israel. Imagine taking the microphone at Fenway Park and telling the story of the Good Yankees fan who helped when all those Red Sox fans walked callously by. Go to Gaza and tell the story of the Good Israeli. Go to China and tell about the Good Tibetan. Go to the Republican National Committee and tell about the Good Democrat. You get the picture. This story is not a page out of *How to Win Friends and Influence People.*

But it does teach us what Jesus means when he commands us to love our enemies. It doesn't mean that we are somehow to muster warm, squishy feelings for those who hate us. It does mean that if they're in a ditch by the side of the road, we stop to help. By using a parable to address loving our enemies, Jesus bypasses an intellectual debate and goes for the right-brain impact of a vivid story.

Jesus also makes his point through his own behavior. In John 4, when Jesus needs to go from Judea in the south back to his northern home, he does not cross the Jordan to go around Samaria. He marches right in and sits down at a well. And it's not a hidden, out-of-the-way well where no one would be likely to see him. He sits at the traditional site of Jacob's Well, important to Jews and Samaritans alike.

While he is there, a woman comes to draw water, at which point he breaks further taboos by engaging her in conversation. Jewish men didn't talk with women in public. When Jesus' disciples come with some food, they don't mention any surprise that Jesus is talking with a Samaritan, but they're dumbfounded that he's talking to a woman. It is, in fact, the longest recorded conversation between Jesus and any other individual in the whole New Testament. Jesus and the woman debate their religious differences, but Jesus pulls back from that to focus on something bigger that can bring them together: "God is spirit, and those who worship him must worship in spirit and truth" (John 4:24).

By going into Samaria, Jesus challenges a behavior toward enemies simply by acting differently. He doesn't first have a dialogue session in the Temple about crossing the border. Neither does he send word ahead to Samaritan officials to ask permission or to find a place for him to make a speech. He just crosses over, sits down at a well, and has a conversation with the first human being to come along. The result? That Samaritan woman becomes the first evangelist in the area. At the urging of her town he stays two days and "Many Samaritans from that city believed in him because of the woman's testimony" (John 4:39–42).

Both in his stories and in his actions, Jesus turns the focus away from the differences and toward their common humanity. Always his instructions and actions are to return hurtful actions with kindness, to pray for those who persecute us, to take an oppressive command like carrying a pack for a mile and going one better to two miles.

Jesus doesn't deal directly with the specific threat of violence. At some points in his ministry as people try to kill him, he avoids them. Of course at the end he allows himself to be executed. When he finds people extorting others, as the merchants in the Temple, he makes a whip and drives them out. But there is no indication that Jesus ever carried a sword or inflicted physical harm on another individual.

GOD WITH SKIN ON

So how are we to respond to the enemies in our lives? The first thing is to see how many of our "enemies" really deserve that label. One of the things the study of enemies makes clear is that we are easily manipulated into identifying someone as an enemy. When the image of an enemy is presented by a nation, group, or individual who stands to benefit by our accepting that hostility, watch out. Remember how the King of Egypt got the people to accept the enslavement of the Hebrews?

Be aware that we are much more prone to see enemies where there really are none if we are stressed—especially if we are economically stressed. It is in the interests of the powerful to make us like who they like and hate who they hate. History overflows with the examples and we are more easily bamboozled than we would care to admit. The success of cults and gangs shows us how easy it is to turn our enemies into our friends and vice versa. Accepting an enemy designation for a person or group without thinking is like loading a virus onto your computer. It will infect your whole life.

So we all need to begin by asking ourselves hard questions. Are my enemies really my enemies? Have I taken the harmful actions of one person and extended that out to that person's family members or coworkers or to those who share that same religion or ethnic heritage? How is it possible for me to hate a person I have never met? Am I carrying forward the grudges of past history? That's where we have to start—by really trying to determine whether a person or group we have identified as an enemy deserves that title. Not because someone else says they deserve it, but from our own experience.

Lots of "enemies" do not deserve that status, as Jesus tried to illustrate with the Samaritans. But of course sometimes we do have actual enemies who both wish us harm and are working actively against us. Even so, however, the relationship with our enemies is rarely one-sided. Because "love your enemies" is a command rarely put into practice, the chances are pretty good that if we have true enemies, we have acted in ways that have kept that enmity going. It's even possible that we were the ones who actually started it.

In my experiences as a conflict mediator in Atlanta, I saw sworn enemies come to the table on a judge's orders and leave at peace with one another. What happened? They simply had a chance to clear the air. Each listened to the hurts and desires of the other, without lawyers or other group members to keep the enemy image alive. They saw each other as human beings, acknowledged their part in the harm caused, and—to greater or lesser degrees—forgave each other. They didn't necessarily leave as friends, but they were no longer enemies.

As I've been trying to illustrate in these pages, this is more than just personal work. It is God's work or, more pointedly, it is God working in and through us. While God can penetrate any barrier, God's MO is to use us to take down as many barriers as possible, allowing God's love to flow unimpeded. Especially if we have taken the name of "Christian," when we designate someone as an enemy, we have also declared that person to be an enemy of Christ. So check your enemies against the enemies of Christ in the Gospels. Sinners were not enemies of Jesus. In fact, he got in a lot of trouble for being their friend. Religious heretics and those of different racial and ethnic groups were not enemies of Jesus, as the Samaritan examples show. Neither did Jesus go around condemning the Romans. He even shared his last meal with Judas.

If your enemy was not an enemy of Jesus, that person cannot be your enemy either. That's not to say we can't get out of the way if she throws something or even end a relationship entirely when violence looms. When the people of his own hometown tried to throw him over a cliff in Luke 4:29, Jesus got out of there fast. You should, too. That is to say that if you return an eye for an eye and tooth for a tooth, you are putting up barriers for Christ's love.

But we don't need to love our enemies only for their sake, or even just for the sake of their souls. There are times, after all, when God seems to us like our enemy. We don't always admit it, even to ourselves, but there are times, especially when tragedy strikes, that we'd like to haul off and punch God in the nose. The Psalms are full of many such outcries, when it seems that the wicked get everything and the righteous get thrown under a bus. Constantly. Most of the book of Job is just such a cry from an innocent guy with all sorts of tire marks from that bus, calling God to account.

If we have practiced loving our enemies—not feeling warm and fuzzy toward them, but helping them out of the ditch when they're in trouble—then we are in less danger of abandoning our faith when it seems like God has become our enemy. When we've learned to help even those who wish us harm and have kept praying for our worst enemies, even from the bunker where we now have to hide, we are much more likely to keep at least the rudiments of faith.

That's the beauty of Job, for me. Job might have responded to God's frontal assault by turning to other gods or becoming an atheist. But he doesn't. Even in the worst of it, Job stays in touch. His prayer isn't pretty, but it is prayer nonetheless, and eventually God answers and restores Job's fortunes, declaring that nothing Job said was sinful. If we have learned to pray for our human enemies, we will find it easier to talk to God when God seems to have dropped the ball. If we have sent a meal over to that horrid woman who did us so much harm because she's too sick to make something herself, we are more likely to keep up the spiritual disciplines that will allow God to speak a further word to us.

Too many people consider Christ their enemy because Christians have treated them as enemies. To be God with skin on for our enemies is about the hardest thing we can do, but it also has the most potential for world-shaking change. It's not about convincing our enemies to be Christian. It's about being Christ for our enemies. It's about not passing by on the other side of the road when they are near death in a ditch. It's about walking across the forbidden border and getting to know the enemy as a human being who needs to draw water from a well. It's about moving beyond the debate over our differences to the dreams of peace we all share.

DISCUSSION QUESTIONS

1. Who are our national enemies? How do we know? What images are used to underscore this?
2. Corporate advertising encourages us to see certain things like age or fat as enemies. Are such enemies valid? What other enemies are created for us through advertising?
3. Do you have any enemies at your workplace? Are there corporate rules about behavior toward that enemy?
4. Describe an experience with an enemy. Have you ever had an enemy become a friend or vice versa?
5. Have you ever seen anyone love an enemy? What did it look like? How did it turn out?
6. If you could wave a wand and turn one enemy into a friend, who would it be? Why? Is there a step you could take in that direction?

Section

3

My Cat Found God on Facebook

*I*n one sense we could say that we have a "relationship" with everything we encounter in life. My cat, Gatsby, not only has a relationship with me but is jealous of my relationship with my iMac. This jealousy is so intense that Gatsby will do all within his power to disrupt the time that my computer and I spend together. From sitting on the printer tray, to walking in front of the monitor, to leaping on my lap and arching his back as I try to use the keyboard, Gatsby expresses his displeasure with my choices.

My computer relationship aside, I'm not going to devote a chapter to pets or inanimate objects. But I do think it is worth considering the ways that we sometimes experience "God with fur on," or scales or fins or leaves or whatever your preference is within the created order. And while the relationship with the computer might be stretching a bit, what about the world of virtual relationships? Relationships that begin online have ended joyously in marriage, tragically in suicide, or simply provided an opportunity to "meet" those around the world that we might never have known otherwise. How do those relationships affect our relationship with God and our faith?

Cultures in many times and places have had a special spiritual role for our ancestors and all those who have come before. In Christian faith we talk about the "communion of saints." Is it fair to call that a relationship? Do we truly live only in the present? Are there relationships in the unseen? As a friend of mine would say, "Sounds very woo-woo." Still, if you think such relationships are outside Christian faith then you haven't read the same Bible I have.

While our human relationships are of primary importance in our lives, I think it may be in relationship to the "other" that we find the closest analogy to our relationship with God. If God were just another person like us, the Christ event would be mostly unremarkable. Holy men and women were martyred before and since. The thing that makes Jesus unique for Christians is the claim that God, who is by nature "other," was willing to take on human flesh and limitations in order that God's will and love might be more clearly known.

While the entire thesis of this book is that God can still be apprehended and comprehended through "God with skin on," the fact remains that human manifestations of the divine are still incomplete and limited, even in the perfection of Jesus. The basic nature of God remains "other." "God is spirit," says Jesus to the Samaritan woman. That means that while learning to relate to human beings is critically important, we are still left with a jump to be made in relating to a Spirit God.

As we learn to be in relationship with the other parts of Creation, we have to learn to navigate non-human forms of expression and need. As we engage in virtual relationships we learn that one person can take on a huge variety of forms and that we can express ourselves with varying degrees of accuracy in the avatars we create for ourselves. When we watch a loved one in the final days of life calling the names and reaching for the hands of long-past family and friends, we begin to wonder if the things we see with our eyes are truly the only things surrounding us.

And isn't that impulse to find something more ultimately what the search for God is all about? Exploring our relationships with those that are "other" may be the salve that finally allows us to see.

God with Fur On

Relationships with the animal kingdom

As I was going through the storm of divorce and illness, I had one refuge. Sheep. Not that I had a whole pasture of them—there were three—but they lived with me on our five acres of land, and when life became unbearable, I would go outside, sit on a bale of hay, and cry on a sheep.

Sheep are, of course, not the brightest lights in the harbor, and I doubt they understood my issues. But there was something about their dumb stare at my distress—that look which seemed to ask, "So are your issues going to affect my food supply?"—that would get me back on track. Yes, I was in horrible emotional pain, but there was more to the world than me and my problems. It wasn't only about me. Interacting with the sheep gave me perspective. The dog, on the other hand, was no help at all. Josey absorbed my emotional state. When I was depressed, he would be in such despair that if he could have used the phone he would have checked himself into a psychiatric hospital.

Those who have never experienced the human-animal bond have missed out not only on an incredible love, but also on a major part of God's provision for us. For many people, animals exist to eat, skin, or otherwise employ for economic gain or medical research. As we have had the humility to admit that some species have skills greater than our own, we are seeing the benefits of rats that can find landmines and dogs that can smell skin cancer. But those who are willing to look even deeper and actually enter into a relationship with an animal have discovered still more.

When my sheep were not listening to my tale of woe, they were sometimes stuffed into a friend's station wagon and taken to a nursing home where they helped stroke victims learn to speak again. It is the relationship between a girl and her horse at Remuda Ranch in Arizona that is so effective in helping those suffering with anorexia to overcome their fears of food. The 2008 film *Underdogs* shows how the faithful and unconditional love of a dog helps prison inmates in Germany learn to care about something outside of themselves and eventually to care for other people.

It is that level of a relational bond, what Jewish theologian Martin Buber called the I-Thou, that moves us from seeing animal life as something over which we simply have "dominion" to an order of beings God claims as God's own (Ps. 50:10) and that God knows personally, down to the last sparrow (Matt. 10:29). There are still those, however, who discount the bond. I have repeatedly counseled with people who are feeling suicidal after losing a pet, a loss often magnified by their religious leaders who dismiss their pain as neurotic or dash their hopes of a heavenly reunion with their pet by declaring that animals don't have souls. I'm sorry, but such a proclamation is beyond the pay grade of even the pope. We don't know the mysteries of God and should not add to the pain of others by declaring what we do not know.

Psychologists define "close" relationships as those that: (a) have a strong influence on our thought and behavior, (b) result in frequent interaction, and (c) have an influence across many diverse areas of our lives.[25] For anyone who has navigated life with a companion animal for a length of time, it is clear that having fur over skin does not prevent an animal from meeting the criteria for a close relationship.

Because I have an online ministry for those grieving the loss of a pet, I hear from many people who describe that grief as being worse than the grief in losing human family members. That says to me that the love felt before the death was also greater than the love for family members. You can claim that such love is misdirected (although I don't believe it is) but there's no basis for denying its power. And if we can form relationships with animals that we describe as closer than that of family, it is likely that those relationships, too, can have an impact on our relationship with God.

THE BIBLICAL WITNESS

The human-animal bond is one of the central metaphors of the Bible. I am talking, of course, about the relationship between sheep and shepherd. In the Old Testament, this is most famously expressed in Psalm 23 and the words spoken so frequently when comfort is needed, "The Lord is my shepherd, I shall not want." While the Psalm has much to teach us about God's care, I think it's more instructive to look at the way the bond between sheep and shepherd affected that Psalm's author, King David.

We know from 1 Samuel 16:11 that at a relatively young age, David was assigned the task of tending his family's sheep. Unlike my own sheep-tending experience, this was not a matter of owning pets or having a hobby. The flocks and herds of the Israelites in David's time (about 1,000 BC) sustained the family. They provided meat, clothing, and currency. To lose your flock was to lose it all. It had to be protected.

While the task of protecting the flock was absolutely necessary, it was neither easy nor appreciated. Both human thieves and natural predators waited for a defenseless moment, moments that come all too regularly when sheep are left to fend for themselves.

Sheep are, as I mentioned, dumb. A friend of mine had a sheep killed by a dachshund. Sheep, when they are attacked, tend to simply offer up their throats for a quick end. If they get turned over on their backs, they can't get up and can die in the desert heat. They wander off.

When I visited Iceland in July of 1981, the sheep of the island were all loosed from their pens for the summer to graze. It was open range. Did they stay in the areas where there was green pasture? Of course not. Time after time we drove through barren lava fields where there was nothing but ashen formations to be seen for miles. And there, peeking out from behind the cooled, black lava stalagmites, were sheep. Nothing green anywhere to be seen.

In 2004 I spent a week on the Scottish island of Iona where sheep outnumber the human residents. A British veterinarian who was also visiting made the comment that "the job of every sheep is to try to kill itself, and it's the shepherd's job to stop them."

Between keeping sheep safe from thieves, predators, and their own stupidity, shepherds in David's time had to live with the sheep. For anyone inclined to think that meant lying back in the grass and playing the pan flute, David's words to King Saul in 1 Samuel 17:34–37 should give pause. When Saul wants to know why the young David thinks he can take on the giant Goliath, who has the entire army of Israel cowering in fear, David simply describes his experience as a shepherd.

> "Your servant used to keep sheep for his father; and whenever a lion or a bear came, and took a lamb from the flock, I went after it and struck it down, rescuing the lamb from its mouth; and if it turned against me, I would catch it by the jaw, strike it down, and kill it. Your servant has killed both lions and bears; and this uncircumcised Philistine shall be like one of them, since he has defied the armies of the living God." David said, "The Lord, who saved me from the paw of the lion and from the paw of the bear, will save me from the hand of this Philistine."

It was the model of the shepherd from David's youth that directed the mission of David the king. He protected his people as a shepherd protects the sheep, and it was natural that when he looked to God for comfort and help, it was the image of the shepherd that came to mind for his most famous Psalm. That background taught him about courage in fighting for those under his care, but it apparently also had its tender moments.

While David never failed to defend his country in battle, he did rather notoriously fail some of its citizens, and even one of his most loyal soldiers. Uriah the Hittite wasn't just any soldier. He was part of an elite group of fighters in David's inner circle known as "The Thirty." While Uriah was away at war, David sent for Uriah's wife, Bathsheba, and lay with her. When she became pregnant from the encounter, David tried to cover it up. He began by bringing Uriah back from the front lines, hoping he would go home to his wife. Before DNA testing, no one would be the wiser about the child's paternity.

But Uriah was too loyal. He came back to Jerusalem at the king's orders but he would not go home to his wife while his fellow soldiers were still in battle. David tried getting him drunk. Didn't work. Rather than face the shame of his sin, David did something even worse. He sent Uriah back to the front lines and instructed his general to pull back from Uriah when he was in the thick of battle so that he would be killed. And so it was. David then took Bathsheba as his wife.

Most people were none the wiser. But God prompts the prophet Nathan to call David to account for his sin. It's not an easy thing to call a king onto the carpet for such actions, especially when there is no public outcry, so Nathan does not take David on directly. Instead he tells a story. A story about a poor man and his one precious ewe lamb (2 Sam. 12:1–6).

"He brought it up, and it grew up with him and with his children," Nathan said. "It used to eat of his meager fare, and drink from his cup, and lie in his bosom, and it was like a daughter to him." Then Nathan told of a rich man who needed a dinner for his guests. Instead of taking from his own flock, the rich man took the poor man's lamb and killed it for their dinner.

David is completely outraged, declaring that the rich man deserves to die. Nathan then turns the tables and famously answers, "You are the man." It has the desired effect. David recognizes his sin and repents.

The story was effective because David could relate to that poor man. As a shepherd, David had learned not only how to protect an economic asset from threat, but also how deep the bond between human and animal could become. We know from David's strong response that he knew what it was like to love a lamb and watch it grow up. Probably he also knew what it was like to lose such a precious friend to a lion, bear, or thief.

David of course was not alone. The experience of shepherds and sheep was such that it worked as a metaphor for kingship for millennia all across the ancient Near East. Five hundred years after David, in the days of Ezekiel, the prophet blasts Israel's kings for being shepherds who feed themselves and neglect the sheep. "You eat the fat, you clothe yourselves with the wool, you slaughter the fatlings; but you do not feed the sheep. You have not strengthened the weak, you have not healed the sick, you have not bound up the injured, you have not brought back the strayed, you have not sought the lost, but with force and harshness you have ruled them" (Ezek. 34:3–4).

Still another five hundred years go by and we hear Jesus say, "I am the good shepherd. The good shepherd lays down his life for the sheep. The hired hand, who is not the shepherd and does not own the sheep, sees the wolf coming and leaves the sheep and runs away—and the wolf snatches them and scatters them. The hired hand runs away because a hired hand does not care for the sheep. I am the good shepherd. I know my own and my own know me, just as the Father knows me and I know the Father. And I lay down my life for the sheep" (John 10:11–15).

It's remarkable, really. Of all the ways that Jesus might have described the intimacy between himself and God, the image he chooses is the intimate bond between the shepherd and his sheep.

Say what you want about the human-animal bond, but don't imply that the Bible doesn't support the notion that such a bond is as close or closer than any human bond. Shepherd and sheep is right up there with father and son, husband and wife in terms of biblical metaphors for God's relationship with human beings.

GOD WITH SKIN ON

Maybe one of the reasons Jesus went to the animal kingdom to describe a relationship with us is because of all our close relationships, that one is the least fraught with the types of betrayals and abuse that can so mar our conception of God's love. Of course from the human side we abuse animals on a vast scale, even those who have trusted their lives to us as pets and love us faithfully through the beatings. From the abuse of factory farms to dog fighting rings to the everyday abuse of pets, our baser nature is on display.

But when you look at the way our pets treat us, there's a halo around each one of them. Okay, except for my cat. The sad fact is that there are those whose only experience of unconditional love on this earth has come from a pet. Family members have abused or abandoned them. Friends have betrayed them, if they've managed to make any friends at all. Teachers put them in the corner. Judges locked them up as their jailors sneered. Spouses abused them. Religious leaders molested them. But when they came home, there was the dog, tail almost wagging off, unable to contain his adoration. It's sometimes the only thing keeping a person alive, the only bridge over the chasm of despair.

For the abused, the forgotten, the lonely . . . and for all of us who feel those things at one time or another . . . God comes like the fog on little cat feet. Or big dog paws. Or delicate bird toes. Or as a little ewe lamb to drink from our cup and become the only experience of totally unconditional love that we've got. To mock or dismiss that bond is not only cruel; it is spiritual malpractice. It may be the only door on which Jesus can knock, the only story that can open truth.

Dismissing the human-animal bond is also, spiritually speaking, a dismissing of ourselves. That we can form a deep and intimate bond with another species is a statement of faith that the God who is vastly "other" can form a deep and intimate relationship with us. That Jesus refers to us as sheep is not especially complimentary. Even with only three sheep I came to learn that sheep are dumb, obstinate, and cowardly, except when a ram is being macho with another ram. They are also incredibly sweet and placid, at least if you're not slow with the sweet feed. But they need constant watching so they don't kill themselves or let someone else do that for them.

We are sheep and God comes to us as our shepherd—another species who has for some odd reason decided to love us and even lay down his life for us. Living that out from the shepherd side was God's mandate for biblical leaders. Remember that God had Moses tend sheep for forty years before sending him to free the Israelites from Egypt. It was good and appropriate training.

To consent to be the steward of an animal—be it dog or sheep or ferret—and to protect and love that animal with all you have is to gain a glimpse of the heart of God. People risk their lives, and lose their lives, for pets regularly. People died in Katrina because they were told they could not take a furry family member with them to a shelter. For them there was no real choice. They stayed faithful to the one who had been faithful to them. Domestic violence shelters will tell you that a large number of women will not leave a dangerously abusive home because of a threat to kill a pet if they leave.

You can fault their choice if you want and say that human life is more valuable than animal life, but they are not making a decision about life. It's a decision about relationship, stewardship, and love and whether betraying that to save your own skin is something you can live with. You can say those who lose their lives in such efforts are foolish. I say it is the foolishness of the Cross. It is the heart of the good shepherd that gives his life for the sheep.

Accepting a role as steward of an animal allows us to know something of the heart of God, and knowing that can help us trust that God will likewise be there for us. That, of course, is the point I want to make about all of these relationships. What we experience in the flesh will more easily transfer to our relationship with God. If I have at least a limited experience of sacrificing for a different species, I am at least a little more likely to believe that the God of the universe would care for me.

In the end, it's about humility. God is God and we are not. We are as different from God as a sheep is from the shepherd. From the beginning, our salvation has rested on the eventual recognition that "All we like sheep have gone astray; we have all turned to our own way" (Isaiah 53:6). The human-animal bond teaches us that we need help and guidance. Just as David needed Nathan's story about the poor man's lamb to see his own sin, so we need to be called back from the lava field where there is no grass.

Our guide in Iceland told us that as winter approaches the shepherds go out into the Icelandic wilderness and call their sheep. The sheep from different folds are in all different places and are all mixed up. But they return to the right fold because they each know their own shepherd's voice. Sound familiar? "He calls his own sheep by name and leads them out. When he has brought out all his own, he goes ahead of them, and the sheep follow him because they know his voice. They will not follow a stranger, but they will run from him because they do not know the voice of strangers" (John 10:3–5).

Unless we have the humility to admit we are sheep, we will feel no need to listen for the shepherd's voice. If we don't understand that the question is not about the relative value of human life versus God's life but is rather about the relationship and the love that God has for us, we are not likely to take the sheep label willingly. We will believe we need no shepherd. But maybe, if we have learned to honestly love a sheep, we will not be so hesitant to take that label upon ourselves.

As I have written this chapter, the dog has asked to go out three times and has barked repeatedly to warn me of the danger of neighborhood children on skateboards. The cat has tried to make the paper tray on my printer into a bed, has walked on my keyboard, and has insisted (loudly) that drinking water from a bowl is beneath his dignity when I can just as well feed it to him directly with a syringe. And yet, I love them with all my heart, as is evidenced by their continued existence.

Perhaps it is just rationalization for my neurotic behavior, but I think that the patience I develop in caring for them helps me trust that God will be patient with me when I exhibit similar behavior. I can admit the times I have not been the brightest light in the harbor without doing damage to my self-esteem because of the many times I lovingly led one of my errant sheep back from adventures in a neighbor's garage. I know the love of a shepherd for the sheep and therefore do not doubt God's love for me.

DISCUSSION QUESTIONS

1. What has been your experience with pets?
2. Do you know anyone who has benefitted from a therapy animal?
3. Do you know anyone who has risked his or her life for a pet? Do you know of a pet that has saved a human being?
4. What do you think is God's purpose for animal life?
5. Is animal life discussed in your faith community or included in it in any way?
6. How does your faith community respond when someone asks for prayer for a pet or expresses grief at the loss of a pet? Is it different for children than for adults?
7. Have you ever seen yourself as unworthy of God's love?
8. Think of either your relationship with your own pet or that of another devoted pet and pet owner that you know. Is your relationship with God similar or different from that?

God on Facebook

Virtual Relationships

One of the defining characteristics of the twenty-first century is the phenomenon of social media. Just when I thought my mastery of e-mail put me in the cool and happenin' crowd, I learned that only old fuddy-duddies use e-mail now. The hip folks communicate through texting, IM, blogs, Skype, and social networks like Facebook, MySpace, and Twitter or visit in virtual worlds like Second Life or multiplayer games like World of Warcraft. I dove in.

As we began to enter the computer age back in the 1980s or so, societal warning bells began to go off. Pundits claimed that we were becoming too isolated, sitting in front of our computers all day and never interacting with other human beings. I beg to differ. I had long conversations with friends and loved ones in the time that it took my cassette tape drive to load programs onto my TRS-80 Model III. But, whatever the truth of that warning, the benefits of the computer were fast putting most other tedious ways of doing business out the window and nobody was about to give that up.

In the meantime, the Internet and its use were expanding. First companies and then individuals were finding it both possible and profitable to express themselves through a webpage, and e-mail allowed us to have instant access to business associates and pen pals around the globe.

After that, it's been hard to keep up. Web*pages* became web*sites*, attachments with pictures enticed more non-business users who wanted to keep up with ever more mobile family and friends. In the world of computer games the graphics engines were improving at warp speed along with faster processors that allowed for interaction with different characters in the game and eventually other players. At least as far back as the Jetsons cartoon that I grew up with in the 1960s, we have wanted a way to see who we're talking with on the phone and the speed of e-mail led us to wonder why we couldn't just "chat" with friends who might be online at the same time we were. Instant messaging was born. Then video conferencing. In 2007 I was able to make a video call to my brother while I was in Jerusalem and he was in Massachusetts. For free.

The point of this chapter isn't to give a history of Internet technology. While I've been using computers since the day I used the computer at my high school (which had punch cards and took up an entire room) to narrow my college search, I'm not equipped to write such a history. My main point is to say that technology is evolving at an incredible pace and that, at least in church circles, the criticisms of its effects tend to be stuck in the last century.

What I hear often in church groups and from related individuals is the notion that technology isolates and that "real" relationships cannot be formed if you're not physically sitting in the same room with someone. I hear that and wonder if the same things were said when the telephone was first introduced. Part of this is fear. If you can have legitimate relationships without having to be in the same physical space, some might question the necessity of the local church. Numbers are dwindling as it is. With the numbers down, the dollars are down while costs are up (in part because we now have to have computers in our offices!), and churches are closing or merging.

I will not say that this fear is a false one. I believe that the coming of the Internet age is bringing as large a cultural shift as the coming of the industrial age—perhaps larger. There was pain in that transition and there will be pain in this one. Once we change the way we communicate, we change the way we do everything in society, and I think that if the church clings to its twentieth-century model, it will become more museum than prophetic voice. Fears are not unfounded, they are just unhelpful.

While this chapter will suggest ways that I think churches can engage the new century, this is primarily a book about relationships, not church models. And in this chapter I want to make the case that virtual relationships are legitimate, real, and even sacramental—the outward and visible sign of an inward and spiritual grace.

Here's a story to illustrate my point. A friend and I were traveling to Israel in 2007. As we converged at JFK Airport in New York City for our flight, she was distraught. A friend, who was a musician in several local bands, had been killed in a motorcycle accident and the wake was at the time of our flight. When we got to Tel Aviv, she went to find an Internet café.

While there, she visited her deceased friend's MySpace page. There in the comments left on his page were friends who had posted their grief within hours of his death. "How can you be gone?" "You're here but you're not here!" My friend went back to that page several times over the next couple of days and discovered that the page was being used to distribute funeral information.

The social network, MySpace, really took off as musicians learned that they could upload their songs and let visitors listen, thus building an audience. So this young musician had "friends" from all over who "knew" him through his MySpace page and his music. Some of those "friends" felt close enough to him to actually attend his funeral, even though they had never "met" in person.

In the meantime, other "friends" wondered in their comments on his page whether the young man's parents would mind if they had a different kind of memorial. The parents were able to respond instantly . . . of course they didn't mind. The page then turned into an organizing tool and soon all three of the bands with which he had played were committed to a memorial concert in his city. It happened within the space of a week. It happened because of MySpace.

Were those not "real" relationships, just because they were formed virtually? What if worship happened organically and spontaneously like that, outside of the bounds of who is a member here or there? Suppose a bunch of people in a Facebook group decide they'd like to celebrate Christmas in the three areas where the group has the most members? Suppose in one group a member's grandfather has an old barn they could use and someone else has a keyboard. If thirty-five people from that group who have never seen each other face to face head out to the barn, sing carols, read the Christmas story, give each other goofy presents and go home—never to gather in just that way or in just that place again—is that church? Has God been there?

Of course the news is not wanting for stories of Internet predators or the horrible tale of a young teen who thought she had made friends with a boy on MySpace and then committed suicide when he turned on her and called her names. Bad enough until we learned that there was no boy. He was a false persona put out there by a mother in the girl's neighborhood specifically to hurt someone who was a rival to her own daughter. Caution, especially where children are involved, is both warranted and necessary. But if there weren't real emotional involvement, there would be no threat. I'm not trying to say there are no dangers. I'm trying to say that such relationships are real and can grow to meet the criteria for a "close" relationship that we examined in the previous chapter.

Not only are people forming relationships with others virtually, but our views of ourselves are also being shaped and expressed. A Stanford study looked at the ways that creating a virtual image of yourself (an avatar) for the online world Second Life affected offline self-perception, at least in the short term.[26] There was a correlation in ways you might expect. People who created attractive avatars displayed more confidence, friendliness, and extroversion than their ugly counterparts. Ditto for height, with the taller avatars winning out.

What was surprising was that their online behavior was then mirrored in an offline segment of the experiment, regardless of whether their avatar's appearance was equivalent to their own. In other words, those with desirable avatars kept their confidence offline, even if they did not meet that description in real life, while the less desirable avatars continued to accept unfair deals offline, even if they could have won beauty contests in real life.

I am one of the thirteen million people who have created avatars on Second Life. I am also one of the eleven million people who play World of Warcraft. Both Second Life and World of Warcraft have their own economic systems. I've learned more about the laws of supply and demand through the World of Warcraft auction house than I ever did in school. I have had several bona-fide counseling sessions in Second Life with those I have "met" through my avatar who, I should add, is about forty pounds thinner than I am.

As my avatars run around the World of Warcraft universe slaying the minions of evil, the chat bar provides a continual feed of player conversation, both general chat and the chat within your particular guild, if you've joined one. What you experience there is not "virtual" behavior. It is real human behavior—the good, the bad, and the ugly. You watch people try to work together as a team and see what happens when someone acts selfishly. You see the real bad eggs that someone eventually reports to the Game Master and you see those folks who simply exist to help others.

With a world divided into two enemy factions that are at war with each other, you also see the range of behaviors when people encounter enemies. I have had those in the opposing faction spit at me and make rude gestures, and I have had others stop what they're doing and help me out of a bind. More than that, I've watched real conversations in the chat bar about whether it is appropriate to help the enemy! You have real conversations, in some setups with real audio.

I've talked with guild members about real-life illness and family issues, about church and religion, and because I have an avatar that is a hot-looking blood elf, I was able to have a conversation with a fourteen-year-old boy from the rural south about the horrors of real war. Because I have a website with a section devoted to those who have lost pets, I have been able to lend a caring ear to people from around the world in their time of deep grief. Because I write a blog about my mother's horrible journey with Alzheimer's, I have "met" people both near and far who share similar circumstances and need someone who understands.

Does that take the place of a face-to-face session with a pastor, therapist, or friend? No. But there are some for whom reaching out to a sympathetic virtual ear builds the confidence to reach out in the flesh. And there are many more who for reasons related to trust, geography, finances, or introversion will simply never open their hearts to someone face to face. Before the Internet revolution there was no help for them. Do they not count?

So where do we find God in such relationships? How can a virtual relationship help us in our spiritual walk? Well, how many of you have actually sat down and had a cup of coffee with God—experiencing God with your physical eyes and ears so that you have to actually pour a second cup of coffee for your guest? Undoubtedly there are some granted that gift of vision, but I'll hazard a wild guess here and say that for most of you reading this page, your relationship with God is closer to a virtual relationship than to any other type of relationship in this book.

How do most of us come to know God? Through signs and symbols and the "avatars" that God chooses. Let's turn for a minute to the Bible.

THE BIBLICAL WITNESS

No, I don't think that there are cryptic passages of Scripture that predict and endorse the Internet. But the Bible does clearly indicate that a direct face-to-face with God is not something to jump at. In most cases, to see God directly is to die. When Moses asks for that privilege in Exodus 33, God replies, "You cannot see my face; for no one shall see me and live." God then continues, "See, there is a place by me where you shall stand on the rock; and while my glory passes by I will put you in a cleft of the rock, and I will cover you with my hand until I have passed by; then I will take away my hand, and you shall see my back; but my face shall not be seen" (Exod. 33:20–23). St. Paul confirms that it is only on the other side of the veil that we shall see God "face to face" (1 Cor. 13:12).

I would argue that the entire biblical history of God's relationship with God's people has been virtual, using a variety of communication techniques and representations to become known to mortals. God shows up to Abraham as three men and to Jacob as a wrestler. God appears to the Israelites as cloud and fiery pillar in the wilderness and angels stand in for God in all kinds of places in both testaments. God speaks through dreams, through human prophets, through writing on walls, through thunderous sounds from the sky, and through "a sound of sheer silence" (1 Kgs. 19:12). I have to believe that if God was up for writing on walls at royal banquets, there would be no divine hesitation to interrupting a corporate meeting with a message on somebody's Blackberry.

God's MySpace page is the Bible itself. There's the self-revelation of the page and a bazillion friends, millions of whom have left comments, both positive and negative, about God's nature, behavior, and page content. Finally, there is the ultimate divine avatar, Jesus, who God used to enter our world. At last, God's Facebook profile had a picture! The story of Christianity over time has been the story of trying to convince others that Jesus was a true representation of God and not some pretender or madman. It's ultimately a matter of faith. We can't prove it. All we have is the avatar and the reputation of the one who sent him into the world.

GOD WITH SKIN ON

There are two extremes in dealing with the online world. One extreme avoids it entirely, believing it to be foolish and danger-ous—a fantasy place where nothing "real" happens. The other extreme jumps in uncritically, believes everything they find there, and assumes a literal correlation to reality. Those are also the two extremes that I find in response to religion: the atheist and the fundamentalist.

I think that learning to navigate the world of the Internet with both a critical eye and a healthy curiosity can help us to do the same with our faith. Not every representation of God is a true one. The many worlds within the pages of Scripture have different interfaces and rules of engagement and the Kingdom of God has its own economic system and ways to deal with enemies.

I also think that learning to deal with others in a virtual world can help us to deal with others in the real world. Social science can't confirm that yet, because the studies are just begin-ning, but if I were a betting woman (which my bishop says I'm not), that's where I'd put my money. I see it all the time in World of Warcraft, which is mostly populated by the young—or at least those younger than me! Most new players learn that it's not cool to whine or to beg for money you could otherwise earn. If they behave selfishly too often or steal from the guild bank, they get booted from the guild—a reputation that often follows them.

If they are threatening or make remarks that are intolerant of others, they can be booted from the game.

On the positive side, patient players overlook small mistakes and help show the ropes to those who are new. They explain how guild promotions are earned, use their skills to craft items for each other, and help those at lower levels with quests. Players learn to work as a team in dungeons that can't be completed except by ten- or twenty-five-person groups. And they get corrected for misspellings. Exhibiting the Fruit of the Spirit helps you socially in World of Warcraft, and I can't image that learning and deploying those traits online wouldn't rub off at least a bit in the offline world.

But what about all the violence? Social scientists are only now beginning to study such things, although a preliminary study at Middlesex University in the UK found that after two hours of World of Warcraft, players aged twelve to eighty-three felt more relaxed and less angry than before their time in Azeroth.[27] After getting over the shock of learning that somebody eighty-three years old was playing World of Warcraft, I saw that those results mirrored my own experience.

I've been killing evil cyber-things in one game or another for over a decade now and don't feel any more prone to do physical harm to any other creature than I ever was. Getting frustrations out in that way may have even saved a parishioner or two! If I were already prone to violence, would such games increase my tendencies? Maybe. I can't say. Would Jesus have played such games? I have no idea. We have zero accounts in the Gospels of Jesus playing any sort of game at all. My observation is that people bring themselves into their online experience. Predators have a new way to find prey; friendly people have a new way to find friends; helpers find ways to help; saboteurs find ways to make life miserable for others.

Advances in technology have brought us new ways of communicating and forming community. First it was the Pony Express, then the telephone. Those technologies each represented things that were lost and things that were gained. With the world of the Internet, we also have tradeoffs, and youth and business have already signed onto the trade. If and how Christians engage that technology will probably be as different as the Amish are from the Roman Catholics.

While it is my hope that seminaries will begin to study the theology and ethics of the medium, I have seen first hand that God can be just as present in our virtual relationships as in our offline ones and equally veiled in both. I am just as likely to be taken to the cleaners by a slick con man online as by the vacuum salesperson at my door unless I develop a more critical eye. It's just that the nature of that eye varies. In face-to-face encounters I have to develop an eye for body language and visual cues and online I have to delete religious messages from rich widows in Nigeria.

God came to us in the flesh, and I don't know anyone who doesn't believe that is still important. But our virtual relationships can help us to cultivate a connection to God that is less physical and more indirect. When you encounter my deadly World of Warcraft Tauren Warrior in all her bovine glory and chat with me, knowing that I'm really the executive director of the Massachusetts Bible Society, maybe you are better equipped to encounter the gang member in a prison cell and remember that he's a child of God. Learning that things are not always what they seem is a critical skill for being able to see God in the least of these, and the virtual world is as good a schoolroom for that lesson as any I'm aware of.

As long as we remain in this life, we don't get to look behind the curtain. We know God only in the ways that God chooses to be known and experienced, which is exactly how we engage the virtual world. Virtual relationships allow us to take what we know from our face-to-face relationships and begin to apply them where the object is a bit less familiar and knowable in different ways. Maybe that will prove to be a helpful step in deciding to take the final leap—to form a relationship directly with a God who is pure spirit.

DISCUSSION QUESTIONS

1. What have been your experiences with the Internet? Have you ever e-mailed or interacted online with someone you have never met in person? How did that come about?
2. What are your concerns about the new technologies?
3. Have you ever posted a profile to a social network like Facebook or MySpace? How about an online dating site? How did you decide what information to share and what picture to show? Have you ever posted something you have regretted sharing with the world?
4. Do you have any virtual friendships that are strong enough to influence your behavior? How do you decide who can be trusted?
5. If you were in a situation in which you felt you needed some emotional help and support, would you be more likely to look for that help online or in person?
6. Regarding violence in games, do you see a difference between killing monsters in a game online and dangerous field games like football or rugby? Is playing cops and robbers with sticks outside different from doing the same online?
7. What "avatars" has God used in your life to communicate with you? Have any of those means of communication made you feel closer to God?
8. Do you think it would be dangerous to see the face of God while still in this life? Why or why not?

God without Skin On

Relationships with the spiritual world

Throughout this book we have looked at our earthly relationships as a means for us to experience God. But there's a large assumption looming behind that theory—the assumption that a relationship with God is actually possible. Obviously, I think that it is.

The notion of a particular God—a god who actually gets involved in human affairs and has very specific preferences within human history and activity—is an important contribution of the Judeo-Christian tradition to the contemporary world's thinking about religion. Belief in God's involvement and preference has been used both to great evil and great good in our world, but the Bible is clearly eviscerated, both in the Old and New Testaments, without the concept.

I have tried to show that we can access that God through our earthly relationships, but that leaves hanging another question: Is it possible to speak meaningfully about a direct relationship with God when God is absent that earthly form—when God does *not* have skin on? Can we have a direct, flesh-to-spirit relationship? That's what this chapter is about.

A 2008 survey of the American religious landscape by the Pew Forum on Religion & Public Life reports that "more than half of Americans rank the importance of religion very highly in their lives, attend religious services regularly and pray daily."[28] Even when you look at those who profess no religious affiliation of any type at all, seven in ten of those folks say they believe in God and a whopping 35 percent of those nonreligious folks pray at least weekly with 21 percent reporting answers to their prayers!

A question I wish the Pew Forum folks had asked is, "Do you have a relationship with God?" I have found that question asked frequently from the pulpit in evangelical circles (more often in the form of whether we have a relationship with Jesus Christ), but I've heard it far less frequently in mainline Protestant or Catholic services.

A Baylor University study bears that out, showing that although nationally 54.4 percent of Americans believe that God is actively involved in the world, almost 30 percent of both mainline Protestants and Catholics believe God is distant. Among evangelical Protestants the number believing in a distant God is just over 10 percent and among members of Black Protestant churches the number who see God as distant from earthly affairs is 0.0 percent.[29]

What I do hear from devout Catholics, however, is a sense of relationship with one or more of the saints, especially Mary but frequently others as well. That connection is buoyed by the Christian doctrine of the "communion of saints." The Catholic Encyclopedia defines the concept as follows: "The communion of saints is the spiritual solidarity which binds together the faithful on earth, the souls in purgatory, and the saints in heaven in the organic unity of the same mystical body under Christ its head," and goes on to say that "The solidarity itself implies a variety of inter-relations."[30]

Now before you Protestants start to object, remember that many of us recite the Apostle's Creed, which includes the affirmation that we believe in the communion of saints. Take the Catholic definition and cut out the reference to purgatory and you'd be hard pressed to come up with a different Protestant definition of the doctrine that we share. Those who believe that life can exist after death, as Christian faith teaches, have a hard case to make in excluding those folks from the world of relationships. The Baylor study also found that over 20 percent of Americans believe it is possible to communicate with the dead. In the northeast, that bastion of the "intellectual elite" where I live, the percentage goes up to almost 30 percent.

Now mix in the experiences of so many people who keep vigil with loved ones during the final days of that person's life. I couldn't find an actual study that recorded such experiences, but I found one thing so frequently in my years in ministry that when a dying person asked me what to expect, I told them what so many others had reported: that loved ones who had gone before would show up to help ease the passage. In my experience those reports were not correlated to a person's religious belief. More than once I was pulled aside at a funeral reception by a family member who had experiences so completely outside of his or her own worldview that they were in crisis. I've talked with hospice chaplains who echo my experiences.

But it's not just about our relationships with God or the souls of the departed. A September 2008 article in *Time Magazine* begins with the incredible assertion, "More than half of all Americans believe they have been helped by a guardian angel in the course of their lives."[31] It goes on to report, "The responses defied standard class and denomination assumptions about religious belief; the majority held up regardless of denomination, region or education." Ask any gift shop owner about people's relationship with angels and I think it will bear out the findings.

Of course angels are just the nice half. There are also those pesky demons. If the Baylor study asked about that, those findings have not been released as of this writing, but a 2004 Gallup poll found that 70 percent of Americans believed in the devil, up from 55 percent in 1990.[32]

There is a prayer in the Greek Orthodox prayer book for the protection from demons. The Roman Catholic Church has an official exorcist and the website religionfacts.com points out "the Catholic Church unequivocally teaches that angels and demons are real personal beings, not just symbolic devices of literature and myth."[33] Any of the folks who believe that the Bible must be taken literally are stuck with the demons as well as blessed by the angels, and I'm guessing that a comprehensive survey on the subject would show only the mainline Protestants free of anxiety over the influence of demons.

Clearly as Americans report their own experiences, the majority of us believe that some degree of relationship with spiritual beings, human or otherwise, is possible. Further, that's not just a theory that we have—a majority of us report having experienced it in some form or other. Skeptics will no doubt point to some psychological disturbance sweeping the nation or some changes in brain chemistry caused by environmental factors. I would point to what the Bible reveals on the subject.

THE BIBLICAL WITNESS

For those who read the Bible literally, defining "truth" as only the kind of truth you get in a textbook, there is no wiggle room. God shows up on earth both in and out of human skin, invites and engages relationship with human beings, and pokes and prods human history toward a particular end. Angels and demons abound (although the latter are much more prominent in the New Testament), long-gone ancestors like Abraham, Isaac, and Jacob are spoken of in the present tense, and Saul gets the witch of Endor to bring the spirit of Samuel back to give him some advice. (We should note that Samuel seems royally p.o.'d about this.)

The author of Hebrews describes us as being surrounded by a "cloud of witnesses," and even Balaam's donkey stops to recognize and obey an angel. The word "angel" in the Bible means "messenger," implying in the very name a relational role. Most prominently there is Jesus, whom John claims is "the word made flesh."

Of course a literal reading is not the only way to interpret the Bible. There are plenty of others who see the Bible less as a book of factual truth and more as a book of spiritual truth. Those folks say that poems are "true" in different ways than history and that parables have a different kind of truth than law. For many Christians Bible stories can be "true" without claiming that they ever happened in history, in the same way that Aesop's fables give us truth, despite the fact that they're made-up stories.

For that group of Christians the challenge becomes how to categorize the kind of truth being told in the passages about spiritual beings. Are they factual realities? Projections by a primitive culture? Symbols of an abstract reality? Metaphors for the human psyche? Once you crack that door, the possibilities can be overwhelming, which is why I think literalism has such appeal for so many.

For myself, I am a United Methodist. Our denomination does not view the Bible literally, but neither are we left to flounder on our own for meaning. Our tradition has a handy tool for sorting through issues of biblical interpretation. We call it the Quadrilateral. For us, the Bible is critically important, but it is not the only place we look for truth.

We believe that God speaks in the Bible but also through three other means: the traditions of the church, the contemporary experiences of the faithful, and the plain sense of rational thought, which is also a gift from God. Scripture, Tradition, Reason, and Experience—the Quadrilateral. We place premium value on what the Bible says, but when we differ about how the words of Scripture should be interpreted, we seek confirmation from the other ways that God speaks in our world. So . . . let's look at the biblical insistence on other-worldly beings through the lens of the Quadrilateral.

We've already covered three of the four. We're asking the question in the first place because of the overwhelming number of biblical references to spiritual beings in every type of biblical literature. The whole narrative of the Bible is ultimately *about* the relationship of God with God's people. That covers the Scripture part.

In the first part of this chapter we looked at the reported experiences of thousands of Americans (the Pew study polled over 35,000; the Baylor study over 1,700) that favor the literal interpretation. People report actual experiences with spiritual beings on a large scale and claim a personal relationship with God. Experience checks out. We've also looked at the various church traditions, seeing that only the mainline Protestants (of which United Methodist are a part!) view literal spiritual beings with skepticism.

That leaves reason. Now listen up, because you won't hear this from me often. I've spent much of my adult life fighting the literal interpretation of Scripture to which I adhered in my youth. I think many of the truths taught in the Old Testament are taught through myth and fable, that human influence is seen as much as the divine hand in the pages of Scripture, and that a strict literalism actually undermines much of what the Bible is trying to teach us. However, *in this instance*, I think that the truth is closer to the literal interpretation than not. And I have reasoned my way there. My thinking goes something like this.

One of the key truths I get from the Creation stories in Genesis is the notion that God did it. I think it took much longer than six twenty-four-hour periods and that evolution may well have been one of the items in God's creation toolbox. But I do believe the underlying assertion that everything we see around us—from other human beings, to the vastly differing ecosystems, to the dog that is currently on my bed barking his silly head off at the person walking by on the street—all of it is made by God. To me that is the only reasonable explanation for the amazing biology and economy of life. To say that it is a random accident is about as far removed from reason as it gets. Monkeys sitting at typewriters didn't accidentally produce the works of Shakespeare. There was clearly an author. Ditto for the created order.

Now, the part of my brain that affirms the sense of a creator for our earthly reality asks, "Why would the God who created 13,000 species of moss for our earthly abode leave the spiritual realm devoid of other beings? Even if you toss in angels and demons, is that realistic for a God who made a world with 561 species of butterfly? That thinking lends some weight to passages in Scripture that begin to show some heavenly diversity. Seraphim and Cherubim, angels and archangels, thrones and power, elders and living creatures all get a mention. In short, from looking at life on earth, there is no reason to believe that life in the spiritual realm should be any less diverse, interdependent, and amazing.

Further, the more I see the importance of relationships here, the more it seems like loving relation to one another is more than just a technique made for earthly existence. It seems like a core principle of God. Church tradition bears that out, especially in those who have sought to unravel the mystery of the Trinity. With our notion of one God that is somehow also three (Father, Son, and Holy Spirit) we see that there are relationships going on within God even before the creation of anything else. "God is love," says it more simply. You can't love by yourself. A loving God implies a relational God.

I'm not trying to reason here for those outside of a Christian perspective. Some may simply deny there is a spiritual realm at all or claim that God is solely contained here within creation rather than existing in any way outside of it. That's a different kind of argument for a different day and probably for thinkers who are more astute than I am. Many of the best throughout history have done it. What I'm doing here is explaining how someone like me, who does not take the Bible literally, comes up with a literal belief in a God who is available for personal relationship and who exists in a realm full of spiritual beings of many types who are capable of interacting with us.

GOD WITH SKIN ON

While Jesus confirms to the Samaritan woman at the well that "God is spirit," we are still very much living in our skin. How do we reflect a spiritual reality and the possibility of relationship with that reality while we remain in our bodies? And how do we reconcile our need for physical contact in forming relationships with a spiritual relationship partner? In good biblical style, we'll take that last thing first.

A key point of this book is that the bridge between our physical world and the spiritual realm is incarnation—spirit becoming flesh. *The* incarnation was the way God emphasized that point (more about that in the concluding chapter), but that event was followed by the encouragement for us to do for each other what Jesus did for us—to be the Body of Christ for the world. By being God with skin on in our human relationships, we help people develop enough trust to walk across that bridge.

That said, it is still an act of faith and not knowledge. We will never have scientific certainty that the world of spirit exists because science is designed to study the material world. It's like insisting that you get the DNA of the wind. Wind doesn't have DNA, but that doesn't negate its existence. It just means we need another way to identify it.

In the case of the wind, we know of its presence because of the effect that it has on trees, windmills, and people from the weather channel who stand outside in hurricanes. Seeing those effects, we adjust our actions to reflect the reality of wind. I would argue that it is no different in our relationship with what is spiritual. We see the effects of such professed relationships on others, which gives us the desire to check it out for ourselves. When we do, our own experiences in the divine wind convince us of its reality.

The fly in the ointment is that some of the effects of a spiritual relationship that we see can lead us to believe that faith is a psychological disorder. When some public religious figures speak, there are lots of people who want to run screaming from the room. So that brings me back to the first question of how we reflect our spiritual relationship in our bodies in a way that points others to God rather than driving them away.

Well, how did Jesus do it? To begin with, he claimed it. From within his Jewish faith, which was very clear on the fact that God was a spiritual being, he laid claim to close relation: God was his father, he said, and to make the point all the more strongly he used the intimate term "Abba." The English equivalent would be "Daddy." I don't think Jesus was making a claim about God's gender or saying that others could not describe their relationship with God in other terms. I think he was saying that he had a relationship with God that was as close as the bond between a son and his loving dad. That he picked the father-son relation is, I think, a testament to Joseph.

After making that claim, Jesus then proceeded to live a public, spiritual life. In that ministry, Jesus was not showy. While people couldn't help but talk about the miracles, it wasn't because Jesus called attention to them. His walk on the water was at night. He fed the five thousand by directing the disciples to distribute a boy's lunch. He turned water into wine without any fanfare, making even the wine steward at the wedding think that the groom had simply saved the best wine for last. When he raised Jairus's daughter, he sent the crowd out of the room. In the Gospel of Mark Jesus told others not to talk about his miracles so many times that scholars have come to call it "the Markan secret." Jesus didn't turn the crowds away to show that he must spend time in prayer. Instead he went up a mountain after they had gone home and spent the night on his knees.

While Jesus taught in public and drew large crowds, he did not put his relationship with God in the limelight. He began the Sermon on the Mount not with "Blessed am I" but with "Blessed are you." He was careful always to point to God and not to himself. Humility is about the size of one's ego, not the size of the crowd. It's about who is given the credit, not the amazing quality of the feat. With Jesus, it was always about God.

One of the biggest reasons that people get turned off by the Christian's claim to personal relationship with Jesus is the way that too many of us use that to claim special privilege for ourselves and to exalt our status over others who have not yet dared to set foot on the bridge. "I have this relationship which entitles me to eternal bliss while you, poor sot, will burn forever" is hardly an inviting approach. That is not how Jesus lived, is not how Jesus taught, and it gives a picture of God so opposed to the one Jesus gave us as to be tantamount to blasphemy. From the call of Abraham onward, the call of God to relationship has been a call to join with God in service to the world. It never was and never is a call to bragging rights.

If we are to live in such a way that others are willing to make the leap from a relationship with us to a direct relationship with God, we don't need to show that we can walk on water. We don't need to scare people into buying fire insurance. We need to show the love for the outcast and the humility in success that Jesus showed. We need to say, "Blessed are you," not "Damned are you." Only then will it seem safe to reach out into the strange world of the spirit.

Jesus claimed it was possible to be in personal, intimate relation to God, showed what kind of life reflected that relationship, and then implied that others could claim such a relationship for themselves. He taught his disciples to pray "*Our* Father, which art in heaven," and at the end of his ministry, Jesus promised, "I do not say to you that I will ask the Father on your behalf; for the Father himself loves you, because you have loved me and have believed that I came from God" (John 16:26–27). By coming to them in the flesh, Jesus was able to successfully reveal the love of God. Once they understood God's nature, he proclaimed that they were prepared to receive that love directly. It was time for them to walk across the bridge for themselves. And they did.

That is the goal of all our relationships—to be in the world but not of the world. We are flesh and blood and have been granted a material life to live. Like children who need object lessons before they can understand abstract realities, we learn from the example of Jesus how to show God's love in the physical stuff of our human relationships.

But we also learn from Jesus that our efforts here have resonance in a world that we cannot touch or see. "Let mutual love continue. Do not neglect to show hospitality to strangers, for by doing that some have entertained angels without knowing it" (Heb. 13:1–2). We are indeed surrounded by "so great a cloud of witnesses," and in the presence of those witnesses, "let us also lay aside every weight and the sin that clings so closely, and let us run with perseverance the race that is set before us, looking to Jesus the pioneer and perfecter of our faith, who for the sake of the joy that was set before him endured the cross, disregarding its shame, and has taken his seat at the right hand of the throne of God" (Heb. 12:1–2).

DISCUSSION QUESTIONS

1. Do you know anyone who has had experiences that seem to point to a spiritual world? What did you think of that?
2. Are there things in your background that would make you more or less inclined to believe such a claim?
3. Does science have a role in validating such experiences? How do we tell who to believe?
4. What do you think happens when we die? Do you still feel a sense of relationship with someone who has died? What connects you?
5. Do you believe in angels and/or demons? Why or why not?
6. What does it mean to you for someone to have a personal relationship with God? Is that your experience? What either attracts you or makes you wary of such a claim?

I Am the Way

"I am the way, and the truth, and the life. No one comes to the Father except through me. If you know me, you will know my Father also. From now on, you do know him and have seen him."

—*John 14:6–7*

Although you would hardly know it from some preachers, this passage from the Gospel of John is not straightforward. To countless Christians it "obviously" means that professing Jesus as your Lord and Savior, i.e. becoming a Christian, is the only way to get to heaven; therefore, non-Christians are outside of God's salvation. But I want you to read those words . . . read it in your own translation if you want . . . and recognize that the interpretation I've just cited is only that . . . an interpretation.

The text itself says nothing about doctrines and there would be no identifiable "Christian" faith for decades yet. Maybe the traditional interpretation is right. But I think there are other possibilities—possibilities that take the text from being one of the most exclusive in the Bible and make it wide enough to embrace the world. Bear with me while we delve into the most philosophical of the Gospels to see what "good news" it might contain for all those "with skin on."

The fourteenth chapter of John is pretty mystical stuff, which is why we turn to it at mysterious times like funerals. What is clear in this chapter and in the surrounding ones is that Jesus,

God, and the disciples all have overlapping identities. John 14:20 says, "On that day you will know that I am in my Father, and you in me, and I in you." Jesus spends most of the chapter reiterating what John said in his prologue about the Word becoming flesh. "Show us the Father," says Philip. You can just see Jesus slapping his forehead in response. "Have I been with you all this time, Philip, and you still do not know me? Whoever has seen me has seen the Father. How can you say, 'Show us the Father'? Do you not believe that I am in the Father and the Father is in me?"

A couple of chapters earlier, in 12:44–45, Jesus gets so frustrated at what people are beginning to mean by "believing in him" that he doesn't just speak, but he cries out, "Whoever believes in me believes not in me but in him who sent me. And whoever sees me sees him who sent me."

Jesus is not a new deity. He's the same God they have always known: the God of Abraham, Isaac, and Jacob. And he's there to proclaim that the God who walked with Adam in the cool of the evening is on earth walking with them still, and has now made a way to walk not simply *with* us but *in* us, so that "I am in my Father, and you in me, and I in you" (John 14:20). So, if believing in Jesus is simply another way of getting to belief in God, then the Jews, who have believed in God all along, are already included.

Later in chapter 17, as Jesus prays for his disciples, he extends that thinking to all who come later. Verse 20 says, "I ask not only on behalf of these, but also on behalf of those who will believe in me through their word." (Reference back to chapter 12 where Jesus explains what it means to believe in him—namely, that it means to believe in God.) He goes on, "that they may all be one. As you, Father, are in me and I am in you, may they also be in us, so that the world may believe that you have sent me." Now all of that is hardly exclusive. In fact, it's such inclusive language that it led the later Gnostics to identify all of us as actually *being* God.

Believing in Jesus, according to Jesus himself, didn't really have to do with him at all. It was about believing in God. And for those who believed in God, there was some sort of mystical unity that put us all together . . . God, Jesus, us, them . . . everybody. If you knew God, you knew Jesus and vice versa, even if one or the other were traveling incognito.

In saying that *he* was the "way," Jesus seemed to be throwing doctrines out the window. To paraphrase, "No, Thomas, there's not some specific belief or practice that is going to get you where I'm going. Faith is about a 'who' not a 'what,' and that 'who' is God, who happens to be embodied in me at the moment, but will soon be embodied in you, too. You will know the way because pretty soon you will be the way yourself. And I will be in the Father, and you in me, and I in you."

Now think about what we've been talking about since page one, that we come to know and love God through our experience of human relationships, and apply it to the text in John 14. "I am the way," says Jesus. Okay. So who is this Jesus? Well, he is the Word made flesh—God in human form. "Those who have seen me have seen the Father," he says. Incarnation. God in the flesh.

Now stay with me here. Suppose you take out the pronoun and instead of saying "*I* am the way," say "*God in the flesh* is the way." To me, that changes the meaning from a way for Christians to slap down other religions to a simple psychological truth. Over and over again I have counseled with people who simply cannot accept the unconditional love of God because they have never experienced such unconditional love in the flesh. Those who have been abused in one way or another or for some other reason have gone through their lives without loving human contact have no bridge to understand the love of God.

Suppose Jesus was saying that to get to know the love of the Father, you need God in the flesh . . . God with skin on . . . God embodied in human form so that we have some earthly way of understanding heavenly things. That makes sense to me. That's what is being said in 1 John 4:20, "those who do not love a brother or sister whom they have seen, cannot love God whom they have not seen." "I in them and you in me, so that they may become completely one."

And if all of that is in any way true, then it is not just Jesus that is the way, but us as well. All of us with skin on have a responsibility to help others meet God in the flesh. I remember as a child hearing my pastor say, "You may be the only Bible some people ever read." I now believe we should take that a step further and say, as I said in the first chapter, "You may be the only Jesus some people ever meet."

If the only way for people to know the unconditional love and grace of God is to experience that unconditional love and grace in the flesh, that means we who profess to be Christ's body in the here and now have got a job to do. It's not about getting people to assent to a doctrine about Jesus. To believe in Jesus is simply to believe that the way Jesus related to those around him represents the way God relates to us—to see in Jesus the life of God.

And that's not exclusive at all. Lots of people of all faiths and of no faith at all see Jesus as the shining light he claimed to be and see his life and teachings as being full of grace and truth. There are plenty of criticisms of the church and religion, but not of Jesus. I heard a comedian once say, "If there was a group called 'atheists for Jesus' I'd be in it!"

To me, when Jesus tells Thomas that he is the way to God, he means all of that. He means that the life he lived shows the way to God. A life that was so radically inclusive of sinners and heretics that it got him killed by the establishment. His statements about being one with the Father are not trying to establish a doctrine of the Trinity but are simply trying to remind people that God comes to us in the flesh—in Jesus most perfectly, and then in those who profess to be his disciples and call themselves the Body of Christ.

To all those who claim to follow the way he set forth is passed the obligation to live in that way themselves: To continue that radical and inclusive love, no matter who hates you for it. Why?

Because it's the only way to the Father. People walk around the earth in incredible pain or just in dull, lifeless existence because they have never experienced God in the flesh. They don't need someone to lay down the Four Spiritual Laws for them. They don't need a detailed understanding of the Creed. They don't need to go to church. They don't need to read the Bible, which is a heck of a thing for the head of a Bible society to say.

They may come to be interested in and enriched by those things, but those things are not the Way. God in the flesh, God "with skin on" is the way. You—us—as the Body of Christ are the Way, just as Jesus was for his disciples. If we do not love others, especially our closest others, as he did—as he still longs to do through us—we have thrown up one more roadblock to their experience of God's love.

Are you a roadblock in your relationships, or are you the way? Are you part of the Body of Christ in name only, or are you God with skin on for others? You may be the only Jesus some people ever meet. Think about it.

Bibliography

BOOKS

Berscheid, Ellen and Pamela Regan. *The Psychology of Interpersonal Relationships.* Upper Saddle River, N.J.: Pearson Education, Inc., 2005.

Buber, Martin. *I and Thou.* Walter Kaufmann, trans. New York: Charles Scribner's Sons, 1970.

Cialdini, Robert B. *Influence: The Psychology of Persuasion.* First Collins Business Essentials Edition. New York: Collins, 2007.

Fiebig-von Hase, Ragnhild and Ursula Lehmkuhl, Eds. *Enemy Images in American History.* Providence, R.I.: Berghahn Books, 1997.

Hendrick, Clyde and Susan S. Hendrick, Eds. *Close Relationships: A Sourcebook.* Thousand Oaks, Calif.: Sage Publications, Inc., 2000.

Reis, Harry T. and Caryl E. Rusbult, Eds. *Close Relationships: Key Readings in Social Psychology.* New York: Psychology Press, 2004.

ARTICLES

Bellows, Alan. "The Soldier Who Wouldn't Quit." June 14, 2006. http://www.damninteresting.com/?p=253>

Biema, David van. "Guardian Angels Are Here, Say Most Americans." *Time* (Sept. 18, 2008). http://www.time.com/time/nation/article/0,8599,1842179,00.html

Blass, Thomas. "The Man Who Shocked the World." Psychology Today, Mar/Apr 2002. http://www.psychologytoday.com/articles/pto-20020301-000037.html

Ciabai, Calin. "Violent Games Actually Make People Relaxed and Less Angry." April 2, 2008. http://news.softpedia.com/news/Violent-Games-Actually-Make-People-Relaxed-and-Less-Angry-82257.shtml

Dell, Kristina. "How Second Life Affects Real Life." *Time* (May 12, 2008). http://www.time.com/time/health/article/0,8599,1739601,00.html

Institute for Studies of Religion, Baylor University. "American Piety in the 21st Century." Spring 2006. http://www.isreligion.org/research/surveysofreligion/

Jenkins, Mark and Steven Floyd. "Trajectories in the Evolution of Technology: A Multi-level Study of Competition in Formula 1 Racing." *Organization Studies* (Nov. 2001). http://findarticles.com/p/articles/mi_m4339/is_/ai_84670645

Leder, Jane Mersky. "Adult Sibling Rivalry." *Psychology Today* (Jan/Feb 1993). http://www.psychologytoday.com/articles/pto-19930101-000023.html

Paulson, Michael. "Americans See Truth in a Range of Faiths, Massive Study Finds." *The Boston Globe* (June 24, 2008). http://www.boston.com/news/local/massachusetts/articles/2008/06/24/americans_see_truth_in_a_range_of_faiths_massive_study_finds/

Pew Forum on Religion & Public Life. "Summary of Key Findings" *U.S. Religious Landscape Survey.* 2007. http://religions.pewforum.org/pdf/report2religious-landscape-study-key-findings.pdf

Rosenthal, Elisabeth. "Troubled Marriage? Sibling Relations May Be at Fault." *The New York Times* (Aug. 18, 1992). <http://query.nytimes.com/gst/fullpage.html?res=9E0CE6D91531F93BA2575BC0A964958260>

Urban, Ewa. "Competition and Interpersonal Conflict in Same-Sex Platonic Friendships." *Hilltop Review: A Journal of*

Western Michigan Graduate Research(2005, vol. 1). http://www.wmich.edu/gsac/hilltop

Winseman, Albert L. "Eternal Destinations: Americans Believe in Heaven, Hell." Gallup Poll (May 25, 2004). http://www.gallup.com/poll/11770/Eternal-Destinations-Americans-Believe-Heaven-Hell.aspx

Zimbardo, Philip. "Stanford Prison Experiment: A Simulation Study of the Psychology of Imprisonment Conducted at Stanford University." http://www.prisonexp.org/

Notes

1. Elisabeth Rosenthal, "Troubled Marriage? Sibling Relations May Be at Fault." *The New York Times* (Aug. 18, 1992): 3. http://query.nytimes.com/gst/fullpage.html?res=9E0CE6D91 531F93BA2575BC0A964958260

2. Alan Bellows, "The Soldier Who Wouldn't Quit." (June 14, 2006). http://www.damninteresting.com/?p=253

3. Harry T. Reis and Caryl E. Rusbult, Eds., *Close Relationships: Key Readings in Social Psychology* (New York: Psychology Press, 2004), 128.

4. Robert B. Cialdini, *Influence: The Psychology of Persuasion.* First Collins Business Essentials Edition (New York: Collins, 2007), 167–201.

5. Thomas Blass, "The Man Who Shocked the World." *Psychology Today* (Mar/Apr 2002); http://www.psychologyto-day.com/articles/pto-20020301-000037.html (accessed Sept. 15, 2008).

6. Ellen Berscheid and Pamela Regan, *The Psychology of Interpersonal Relationships* (Upper Saddle River, N.J.: Pearson Education, Inc., 2005), 153.

7. Ibid, 203.

8. Ewa Urban, "Competition and Interpersonal Conflict in Same-Sex Platonic Friendships." *Hilltop Review: A Journal of Western Michigan Graduate Research* (2005, vol. 1.), 1.

9. Mark Jenkins, "Trajectories in the Evolution of Technology: A Multi-level Study of Competition in Formula 1 Racing" (May 1, 2008):1; http://findarticles.com/p/articles/ mi_m4339/is_/ai_84670645 (accessed January 11, 2009).

10. Urban, 5, 1.

11. Cialdini, 180.

12. Ibid, 181.

13. Urban, 5.

14. Cialdini, 179.

15. Blass, 1.

16. Philip Zimbardo, "Stanford Prison Experiment: A Simulation Study of the Psychology of Imprisonment Conducted at Stanford University"; http://www.prisonexp.org/ (accessed Sept. 29, 2008).

17. Ragnhild Fiebig-von Hase and Ursula Lehmkuhl, Eds., *Enemy Images in American History* (Providence, R.I.: Berghahn Books, 1997), 3.

18. Ibid, 25.

19. Ibid, 48.

20. Ibid, 25.

21. Ibid, 27, 3.

22. Ibid, 83.

23. Ibid, 32.

24. Ibid, 51.

25. Berscheid, 155.

26. Kristina Dell, "How Second Life Affects Real Life," May 12, 2008; http://www.time.com/time/health/article/0,8599,1739601,00.html (accessed June 3, 2008).

27. Calin Ciabai, "Violent Games Actually Make People Relaxed and Less Angry"(April 2, 2008); http://news.softpedia.com/news/Violent-Games-Actually-Make-People-Relaxed-and-Less-Angry-82257.shtml (accessed July 8, 2008).

28. Pew Forum on Religion & Public Life, "Summary of Key Findings" (U.S. Religious Landscape Survey, 2007); http://religions.pewforum.org/pdf/report2religious-landscape-study-key-findings.pdf (accessed Sept. 20, 2008).

29. Institute for Studies of Religion, Baylor University, "American Piety in the 21st Century" (Spring 2006); http://www.isreligion.org/research/surveysofreligion/ (accessed Sept. 20, 2008).

30. http://www.newadvent.org/cathen/04171a.htm (accessed Oct. 5, 2008).

31. David van Biema, "Guardian Angels Are Here, Say Most Americans," *Time* (Sept. 18, 2008); http://www.time.com/time/ nation/article/0,8599,1842179,00.html; (accessed Sept. 30, 2008).

32. Winseman, Albert L. "Eternal Destinations: Americans Believe in Heaven, Hell." Gallup Poll (May 25, 2004). http:// www.gallup.com/poll/11770/Eternal-Destinations-Americans-Believe-Heaven-Hell.aspx (accessed July 17, 2008).

33. http://www.religionfacts.com/christianity/beliefs/ angels_demons.htm (accessed Oct. 1, 2008).